How To Help Your Child SURVIVE & THRIVE In Public School

D0173077

How To Help Your Child SURVIVE & THRIVE In Public School

Cliff Schimmels

Fleming H. Revell Company
Old Tappan, New Jersey

Scripture quotation is from the New American Standard Bible, © The Lockman Foundation 1960, 1962, 1963, 1968, 1971, 1972, 1973, 1975.

Excerpt from "The Death of the Hired Man" from THE POETRY OF ROBERT FROST edited by Edward Connery Lathem. Copyright 1930, 1939, ©1969 by Holt, Rinehart and Winston. Copyright ©1958 by Robert Frost. Copyright ©1967 by Lesley Frost Ballantine. Reprinted by permission of Holt, Rinehart and Winston, Publishers.

Library of Congress Cataloging in Publication Data

Schimmels, Cliff.
  How to help your child survive and thrive in public school.

    1. Home and school—United States. 2. Public schools—United States. 3. Education—United States.
I. Title.
LC225.3.S34   371'.01'0973   81-21007
ISBN 0-8007-5135-3   AACR2

Copyright © 1982 by Cliff Schimmels
Published by Fleming H. Revell Company
All rights reserved
Printed in the United States of America

CONTENTS

Introduction
"Whose Hair Is It, Anyway?"

At twenty-six years of age, I was a football genius. I knew I was a genius because I had just persuaded a school board in a small town in western Kansas to employ me as their head football coach. So, early in August I moved to that town, carrying with me all my prized possessions: my young family, my frequently read Darrell Royal football book, an organized system of X's and O's that I had pieced together largely from notes on coffee shop napkins, and my dreams. Dreams I had in abundance, and I cherished each one dearly. Secretly but vividly I had planned the next two decades. I had already practiced my acceptance speech for the time when I would be chosen the town's "Man of the Year." I had rehearsed the humbleness required to shake hands with an opposing coach whom I had just beaten by four touchdowns. I had lost a few pounds so I wouldn't be such a load when my players raised me to their shoulders and carried me off the field. I was ready to coach football.

About a week before the first practice, I got my initiation. I was sitting in my office dreaming and planning when the principal called to tell me that I was about to be visited by the father of one of the players. Although I was prepared, I prepared a bit more.

He walked in and sat down as if he owned the place—taxpayers sometimes act that way. "You the new football coach?" he asked.

"Yes, sir." I don't think he detected the trembling in the voice. But I couldn't tell. He wasn't showing much emotion.

"What are you going to do here?" He never really looked at me when he asked.

But that was a question I could get into. "Well, I am going to implement a Wing T offense with a man in motion and a flip-flop line. We'll have a lot of power on the corners, but we will still be able to get three receivers out quick."

I was just getting warmed up when he interrupted, "Is that all?"

I quickly surmised that he was not offense-minded, so I took a new twist. "No, not at all. I am going to put in the stack-4 defense with a lot of stunting. As far as I know, no one in the area is running such a defense, so we should really have surprise on our side."

He interrupted again, "Anything else?"

By now, I was about to exhaust my repertoire of both dreams and plans, so I dug a little deeper and answered, "Well, I do have a very elaborate off-season program planned. We will combine running, weights, and isometrics, and we will spend a lot of time just thinking football."

He still wasn't impressed. "Yeah?"

"Well, I do intend to teach the young men a lot about personal integrity and sportsmanship and playing the game with a positive attitude to maximize the fun aspect of good, hard-nosed football."

"I just hope you can get my kid to cut his hair. I've tried everything and he refuses to do it." And with that, my guest got up and walked out.

Who Owns the Child, Parents or School?

In those few minutes, I learned the most important lesson I have learned in more than twenty years in the dual professions of teacher and parent. In that wonderful world between infancy and adulthood, the human being is subject to various influences, forces, or powers. And frequently those forces are uncoordinated, inconsistent, and even contradictory in their intentions, instruction, and expectations. No wonder our children are confused and undereducated.

As I sat in that football office with the tips of my ears the color of pickled beets, I realized that perhaps parents and school people ought to get together more often than they do. I learned that I could never become a very effective teacher until I had some sense of what was happening to the child at home. I also learned that I could never become a very effective parent until I understood what was happening to the child at school. But too often there is an unfortunate gap between those two agencies.

My first impulse is to fix blame for that gap. I could begin by blaming myself and all the other young coaches and teachers who begin their educational professions with so much idealism that sometimes they refuse to see the everyday, practical concerns and possible solutions. Or I could blame that father for his willingness to pass off some of his parental responsibility to an outside agency. But fixing blame is a hard task.

Like the six blind men of Indostan who went to see the elephant, we were both partly in the right and both entirely in the wrong.

Young teachers do have a right to be idealistic, to think they can change the world, alter community direction, and make rain come during droughts. And parents do have a right to expect something to happen in the schools.

But as educators and parents spend their time pointing accusing fingers and wondering what each can expect from the other, there lurks in the wings the most important character in this dramatic conflict, that long-haired football player. Somebody has to worry about him, his physical, emotional, spiritual, and moral needs.

To personalize this, ask yourself who, in fact, are you willing to trust with the authority to tell your own child to cut his hair? (I realize this is a rather outdated example, but I like it because it does indicate something very dear to the child. Most young people have a healthy respect for their own hair.) Who is going to provide the information, the knowledge, the understanding, the love, the commitment, the discipline, and the example needed to enable your child to grow into the personhood for which God has ordained him?

Let me assure you that somebody has to provide those things and has to provide them in such a way that your own child can accept them. Without going into the full-blown details of a things-are-rotten speech, let us agree that for thousands, yea millions, of young people in this country, things are rotten.

There have never been many guarantees in child rearing. There are even fewer now. The secret to success is hidden somewhere in how the parents and the school can coordinate their efforts so that the child can sort through the messages and find some direction. That is what this book is about.

Why Do I Care?

At first glance, you may wonder whether I am motivated by harsh feelings. You may think I am still unhappy about being left speechless and dreamless in that football office years ago, that my bitterness has finally burst into an overt pronouncement of what I, as an educator, have always wanted to say to parents if I had the courage. But that's not so. At least, I don't think that is the situation. Rather, I am interested in your child and his development. I like children and have chosen teaching children as my life's work. I am pleased with that decision. But if you are skeptical about my motives, let me remind you that my happiness and your happiness depend on how smoothly your child and other children pass through childhood and adolescence into adulthood.

I was driving my car on a busy expressway when it occurred to me that the people piloting those lethal weapons whizzing by had learned their ethics in schools or at home.

Every time someone cooks our meals in a restaurant, adds up our bills at the supermarket, programs the bank computer, drives on our streets, or votes in an election, you and I become consumers of the products of child-rearing agencies.

Those statistics about low reading scores, declining test scores, or the percentages of failures of minimum competency tests are more than figures. They are of vital concern to anyone who lives in this country, is fed from its soil, is heated by its energy, drinks its water, or breathes its air. To paraphrase John Donne, every person's ignorance or educational inadequacy diminishes us, our happiness, and our abilities to fulfill our roles in the Kingdom of God.

If people stop reading, the newspapers go out of business. If people fill their aesthetic hunger with visual trash, then visual trash dominates our television screens. If people are disinterested in world and national affairs, then scoundrels become our statesmen and public servants. There are two major forces responsible for a stable future—parents and schools—and I want to make sure both are functioning.

The Biblical Mandate

In Deuteronomy, God, through the voice of Moses, established the principles of a culture that has survived more than 3,000 years. In the sixth chapter, God ordains the plan and the institution by which that culture is to be perpetuated and propagated. And what is that institution with such a holy and responsible task? Is it a great church? A system of government? An international communication system? No. For a task that important, God ordains the office of parenthood. He says, "And these words, which I am commanding you today, shall be on your heart; and you shall teach them diligently to your sons and shall talk of them when you sit in your house and when you walk by the way and when you lie down and when you rise up" (Deuteronomy 6:6, 7).

Modern parents might protest that the injunction should be generalized, that God is suggesting only that the older generation should teach the younger. But that is not the way the ancient Israelite read the mandate, and that is not the way the Apostle Paul reaffirmed it in his Epistles.

Where Do Parents Start?

Let me make some assumptions about you and your relationship to the mandate. The first is that your child is the most precious possession you have, and that you realize this. I hesitated before using the word *possession* because I was afraid that would put the child on the level of a new pair of shoes or a used station wagon. I don't mean that, not even by implication. I don't even mean that you put your child on the level of a profession or a philosophy of life or a set of beliefs. But during your lifetime you are going to invest your energy, time, creative wisdom, judgment, decisions, and moral integrity in a variety of projects and possessions. Among those—job, house, bank account, or whatever—the only one which is going to survive you and represent you as a significant force in this world after you have left it is your child. His rearing deserves some attention.

The second assumption is that you really *do* want the school to be successful in relating to your child's needs. Don't be too shocked by that statement. After several years of counseling with parents and students, I have concluded that some people are actually hoping the school will fail. I guess they like saying, "I told you so." I am not jesting. Examine yourself; see if you can honestly trust the school and are willing to give it the credit for its role in the positive development of your child. Be careful. I am asking for some self-examination that could be painful. Are you prepared to say something like, "I really like the way the coach got my son to cut his hair." Are you prepared to admit, "The teacher succeeded where I failed." It takes some parental nobility to admit this, but I want to assume that you are a noble person.

The third assumption is that you are willing (perhaps I should say excited) to accept your full responsibility in the education of your own child. In this age of specialization, that assumption may not be as valid as I suppose. One of the conveniences of living in the posteverything age is that we have some agency to take care of every phase of human living; but more importantly, we have someone to blame for failure in any phase. If I am not as handsome as Burt Reynolds, it's my barber's fault. If I have a heart attack, it's my doctor's fault. If the automobile doesn't operate efficiently, it's the mechanic's fault. If my child doesn't know how to read or gets pregnant or in any way offends his or her parentage, it's the school's fault. By the same logic, if my soul goes to hell, it's the preacher's fault. Excuses carried to the extreme inevitably reach the absurd.

In spite of how good or bad schools may be or can be or should be, the frightening truth is that you have as much responsibility in educating your child as anyone. I am assuming that you want your child to read, to write, to score well on standardized tests, and to demonstrate other indications of having been educated. But I am also assuming that you are willing to make some sacrifices of your own time and talent to see that this happens.

With the rise in private and Christian schools in recent years, many parents have been given more choice in where their children attend school. It is good that parents should have this choice, and it is also good that public schools do not have a monopoly on children's education. But the very existence of this choice places an unusual responsibility on parents. They now must know enough about the whole, wonderful process of education to be able to make a wise decision. Don't be deceived. Make a careful and systematic assessment of your child's school—of its philosophy, the teaching techniques, the probability of success, the inducements to learning, and the lifelong possibilities it offers your child.

If, after that assessment, you decide the school is not right for your child (be careful, you are dealing with a young person's life—twenty, thirty, fifty years) find another school which will offer him what he needs. But be sure. Just because a school *claims* to be something doesn't mean that it is. Different is not necessarily better. Some schools which have originated in recent years are not sound in their educational approach, are staffed with poorly trained and poorly paid teachers, and greatly limit the future decisions of the graduates. Now that you have the choice, you must accept the responsibility to be able to make a wise decision.

But your responsibility does not end there. Even if you choose to send your child to a nonpublic school and make the financial sacrifices needed to keep him there, you are fulfilling only part of your duties as a parent. Although you may be paying double taxes for schooling, you are still the single most important educational agent in your child's life. If you reject this responsibility your child's growth will be retarded, and both of you will have to live with the consequences.

What Are Schools For?

But you may protest, "I don't know how to make a systematic study of a school, and I don't have any idea what other parental duties I should perform." Well, you have come to the right place. That is exactly what the first part of this book is about. I will report my observations of schools, gathered from twenty years in various teaching assignments and schools. I will help you develop some criteria, based on these observations, for judging the soundness of a school, and I will enumerate in clear terms where the school—any school, your child's school—is inadequate or helpless and must have your support.

Chapter one begins the emphasis on the role of the individual teacher in the educational process. It won't take much reading between the lines to ascertain what I think is important. If you want your child to go to a good school, send him to the one with the best teachers. If you want your child to have a positive experience, make sure he always gets a good, thorough, understanding teacher. Oh, how I wish it were always that easy!

Chapter two focuses on different approaches to teaching. It introduces you to four types of teachers and tells you how each responds to certain aspects of the educational process. From this discussion, you should be able to develop some kind of strategy for assessing what kinds of teachers are available and what kind would be best for your child. In this chapter, I will warn you about the hidden as well as the visible lessons a teacher communicates.

Chapter three is more specific. I will develop criteria for evaluating individual teachers, and I will suggest some techniques you may employ to attempt to correct weaknesses and errors. Far too often, concerned parents with valid causes lose their effectiveness because of the way they approach the problem. In many cases, their efforts are not only ineffective but counterproductive. There is a right way and a wrong way to fight city hall or the school or even naive football coaches.

The suggestions in this chapter are tempered by a teacher's point of view. At least I know how *I* like to be approached. You can be an effective force if you don't begin by putting teachers on the defensive.

Chapter four is actually a transitional chapter. It will conclude the section on school and introduce the section on the family by discussing the school's limitations. In recent years, the school has been asked to do some jobs which had previously been done by other institutions such as family and church. The school has not been too effective with its new responsibility; and, in some cases, it has even lost sight of its traditional function. By reminding you of the school's inherent inadequacy in these areas, I am at the same time reminding you of your obligation as a parent.

What Are Families For?

For all parents of school-age children, there is one inevitable rule of life. Every day has a three-thirty, or whenever the school's dismissal bell rings. It is then time for a sometimes faltering, nebulous institution called the family to assume its direct responsibility for the education of the child. Since you adults are by age the mature force in your family, you are the ones who need to think about doing it right.

The second part of this book is dedicated to that purpose—to help you think about how your family works as an educational agent in your child's life.

Chapter five contains a discussion of the family structure with emphasis on the nucleus or hub, which must be present in all united, working families. You'll find some definite suggestions for discovering that nucleus or creating one if none exists naturally.

Chapter six deals with the importance of the family as a teaching institution. Here I have enumerated some crucial, abstract lessons which your child must learn at home if he is ever to learn them. Again, these remarks have been tempered from a teacher's point of view. I am basically telling you what every educator would like for you to teach your child. These lessons are quite fundamental to life, to your child's whole development. If you do not teach them to him, he will probably never be as complete as he was created to be.

Chapter seven deals with a specific role for the family—supplementing the teacher's efforts in the area of academic content. Sometimes, the job doesn't get done at school. You can look for reasons, go to the board meetings and shout, or sue the teacher; but your child still doesn't know how to read or multiply. You will probably have to be a supplementary teacher at some time during your career as a parent. Chapter seven contains definite suggestions for doing the job.

What Are Friends For?

As I have watched my children grow through the years, I have learned to hate a few juvenile utterances. At the top of the list is the classic, "But Daddy, everybody else is doing it." Yet, despite all my hatred for it and all my attempts to prove the statement's logical fallacies, it still carries an important message: The peer group is a powerful influence in the lives of most young people.

This is the thesis of the third part of this book. Here there are three chapters, one on friendships, one on extracurricular activities, and one on drugs, sex, and alcohol. At first glance, this may seem to be an unusual grouping, but it really isn't. In fact, those three topics are more interrelated than we sometimes suspect, and it is this interrelatedness that deserves our attention. Extracurricular activities will provide your child with one dominant source of friends, yet his friends will influence his selection of extracurricular activities. And his friends will definitely influence his attitude toward drugs, sex, and alcohol.

This whole issue of peer pressure requires diligent, wise, judicial guidance and sincere prayer. It is here that the parents and the school have mutual concerns and frustrations. It is here that the school and parents must work together and must depend on each other.

The information in this part of the book is largely based on the mistakes I have seen parents make, and I find that admission frightening. But if we have to learn difficult lessons from mistakes, I would prefer to learn them by observation rather than by direct experience.

What Are You For?

Finally, the book ends with a summary chapter which reminds you that your school is a dynamic, changing institution and that you can be instrumental in determining the direction of that change. Regardless of how mysterious the school system may appear to be, it is still a grass roots government that is operated by local citizens just like yourself. If you don't like the way things are going or if you are frightened about the way they might go, you have the right and the opportunity to make yourself heard. All you have to do is learn the correct procedure.

The glossary at the end should at least be entertaining if not informative.

This is the content of the book. If you are a parent, God has entrusted you with a rare privilege, the privilege to direct a life through its formative and crucial period. Like any other important task, there is always a risk.

There are various powers or influences that come together in that one single life: the school, the family, the peers. It is my thesis that one of the important roles of the parent is to see that those powers speak as one unified voice.

Yes, sir. How short would you like your son's hair to be?

PART I

THE POWER OF THE SCHOOL

He had become such a part of me. I had not really intended for it to happen that way, but it did. I had seen those overindulgent mothers before, and I had promised myself that I would never become one. Nevertheless, he grew into a part of me, and I like to think that I grew into a part of him. Even when he was little, I enjoyed watching him form his personality. I entertained myself for hours just by studying his facial expressions—the way he fixed his mouth when he was determined, the way he looked into space when he was frustrated, the way his eyes glistened when he was delighted. I appreciated his inquisitiveness, his creativity, his sweetness.

I don't know whether he knew what he was doing, but somehow he learned to complement me as I went through each day. He knew when I was pensive and needed silence. He knew when I was lonely and needed his affection or needed to show my affection. He knew when I was jolly and needed his antics to amuse me.

We became quite a pair, the two of us—mother and son—carrying each other through each day and making it all worthwhile.

Well, I knew that inevitable day would come and, on the outside, I looked forward to it. My husband and I had talked about it for months. This was a highlight, a benchmark, one of life's major milestones. But when that big, yellow bus finally rolled up outside our yard and honked that blasted horn, I realized I wasn't prepared for all the emotions I was going to feel for the next twelve or thirteen years. For one thing, the bus looked so huge and impersonal; and when he climbed up those steps with his tiny legs filled with purpose and he disappeared into the bowels of that bus, I felt that I would never see him again—at least never as he was before. We would never be that way again. Now I must trust him to people I don't even know. Sure, they all came with the best of credentials; but still, how long would it take them to learn to read the mouth and the eyes and the gaze? How long would it take them to realize that he could respond to their moods and help them through their day, or would he lose that and become callous to other people completely? And if he lost that, what else would he lose over the next decade?

I must confess, I sat down and cried. A part of me died that day when I sent my son to that unknown, alien world called school. A part of me died, and now I have to fight feelings of jealousy and fear and distrust. I really want to be honest with the schools. I want to give them their chance and their credit, but I want those people to understand that I have entrusted them with a precious part of myself. I want them to respect that, too.

*   *   *

Since you are reading this book, you have probably already experienced some of the happiness and frustrations this young mother describes—the hollowness of that first day, the helplessness which comes when you realize your child is going to spend 6 hours a day, 180 days a year for 13 years in that other world, in the hands and care of people you may never meet. And all in a situation over which you have very little control. It is frightening, at least for any parent who deserves the title of parent.

I don't propose to alleviate all your fears for you, and I am not going to be dishonest about the power of the school in your child's formation. But I don't think the school world has to be all that foreign.

Schools and school people aren't really as mysterious as they may seem. In fact, some are nice folks once you get to know them. I offer the next four chapters as an introduction. And let me assure you that after having spent most of the last two decades in schools, I have become rather confident about what they are doing with my own children.

1

"Hey Teach, We Gonna
Learn Anything Today?"

Exhibit A. The third-grade class had just finished a lesson on the planets. The students had read all about planets in their *Weekly Readers*. Since there were various levels of reading competence in the room, the teacher walked quietly about during the silent time. She was armed with gentleness and a quick smile as she would stop and help a student through a more difficult passage. Finally, all students had completed the reading and were sitting quietly with their readers folded on their desk tops.

The teacher, still mobile and still graciously armed, began to ask questions. At first, only the hands of the brighter, more aggressive students flew to the air for recognition; but soon, the sequence of questions built to a climax as more students began to plead for an opportunity to respond. The teacher went slowly, but with enthusiasm. Each student's answer was rewarded with a comment, a smile, and perhaps an added thought. If a student wanted to add to an answer from one of his colleagues or wanted to ask an additional question, he was given the time and the climate to conclude his investigation. Each child in the room volunteered some kind of oral participation during the lesson. Time flew quickly. Excitement mounted, and at the conclusion those students could name and spell the planets, could place them in their order from the sun, could explain their rotation, could explain the meaning of days and years on earth, and could recite several characteristics about each of the other planets.

When they were finished, the teacher thanked them for their response and rewarded each with a Mars bar. Everybody seemed to think it was appropriate.

Exhibit B.   The algebra class was stumped. The student had just written his problem on the chalkboard. He had shown all the necessary steps toward solution and had circled the number which represented the right answer.

The teacher asked, "Is that the right answer?"

"Yes," the student responded.

The teacher furrowed his brow as if in thought and then asked, "If that is the right answer, what does it mean?"

The student was stumped and slightly irritated. "What kind of question is that? All my life I have been taught just to find the right answer, so that's what I did. What do you mean, 'What does the right answer mean?' "

The teacher disarmed him with a grin, but continued the questioning, "Students, that is not good enough. There are many problems in life which may have a right answer, but just finding the right answer is not good enough. It is not enough to find the right answer to the energy question. We must know why that is the right answer. Now, who can help him out? What does it mean to us that this is the right answer?"

The room was filled with a busy silence. Eyes narrowed as they studied the writing on the board and mouths curled into inquisitiveness. Twenty-nine minds focused on the question, What is the meaning of the right answer? The teacher waited patiently for what might have seemed too long for a less-informed educator.

Finally, one student offered a possibility. With gentleness but a commitment to the discovery of meaning, the teacher began the questioning anew. Throughout the rest of the period, the students applied the test of "why" to their right solutions. They confirmed algebraic equations, they pursued mathematical theories, and they pondered the meaning of *meaning*. During that time, there were no discipline problems, no horseplay, no harsh words, and no disinterest.

Exhibit C.   The classroom was in chaos. When the bell rang, the students wandered in, listlessly and casually. Some made it before the tardy bell, but most didn't. The teacher sat in the front of the room at his desk and called the roll without looking up. After each name was called, a student answered with a perfunctory "Here." However, in a few isolated cases, their "here's" came weakly, after an embarrassed silence, accompanied by nervous giggling which certified that it was bogus.

Still sitting, the teacher taught for the day. "Okay. Read the next chapter in your book and answer the questions at the end. We are going to have a test on it Friday."

Someone asked, not completely interested, "Which chapter is it?"

Another student asked, "Do we have to hand in the questions?"

"If you want a grade for them, you do."

Again, a student asked, "Are we going to get back the questions we handed in last week?"

"Yes," the teacher answered.

"When?" It was more of a dare than a question.

"When I get them graded; that's when. What do you people think I am, anyway? I have things to do, too. Now shut up and get to work on the next chapter." With that, the teacher picked up the sports magazine from his desk and proceeded to flip through it, pausing occasionally to check the progress of the class through the vantage point of his feet resting on the desk top.

A group of boys congregated in one back corner, watched a student carve a dirty word on the desk, talked coarsely, and laughed vulgarly. A small group of girls occupied the other back corner and practised the art of cosmetics—brushing hair, painting nails, dabbing eye makeup. Two eager-looking young men sat in the middle of the room and played a computer game. Another student read the newspaper. A few scattered throughout the room read silently about the sequences which had led to the war which was to end all wars.

All students adjusted to their various activities in such a way as to suggest this was standard procedure.

The Unsystem

First, let me assure you that the stories are true. In a one-week period, I observed each one of those, all in the same district—the latter two in the same building. So what is the point? Simple. Considering the diversity in approaches and in enthusiasm which individual teachers bring to their classrooms, it is rather difficult to make any generalizations about the school system. In fact, in actual practice, there *is* no such thing as a school system.

I hear those gasps and groans which come anytime a sacred cow is slaughtered, but I am prepared to defend my position. When one thinks of schools, it is a mistake to think in terms of a system.

I realize the natural tendency to think that way. It is comfortable, particularly if one aspires to be a reformer. It is easy and safe to criticize a system. All of us have learned that systems are corrupt, that they are insensitive, and that they are open to criticism. That is part of the American culture. You can criticize the system all you want without really hurting anybody. You can blame the system for all your miseries, yet never be faced with the threat of confrontation. A system is impersonal. No one is the system, so you can even criticize the system to the man in charge without ruffling feelings.

Besides, it is more fun to plan an attack against a system. You can marshal your forces, manipulate your divisions, and carry out nonpersonal wars. Like Patton in Germany during World War II, you can engage in a battle of wits.

Unfortunately, the schools are not an organized movement like the German army during the 1940s. They are a guerrilla outfit, and any conquering and successful reforming must be rooted in consideration of this basic characteristic.

The federal constitution supports my claim. That document is silent about the subject of education; thus, the process becomes, by implication of omission, one of the states' rights under the Tenth Amendment. Thus, there are at least 50 different school systems in the United States. But in each state there are districts—more than 16,000 across the nation—with individual boards, individual needs, individual moods, and individual values; so each district becomes a system. Within each district, each building has an unique personality, a spirit or attitude that distinguishes it from all the other buildings in that district and makes it a system unto itself. Within each building, each classroom teacher has an individual style, likes and dislikes, specific emphases, a manner of response, a special approach to the art of living. And this is the culprit or the cause! For your child, the system of education in the United States is defined by what happens in *one classroom.* If that teacher is good, or your child perceives him to be good, then the educational system is good. If that teacher is inadequate and insensitive, then the educational system is bad.

I realize this is discouraging talk coming from an educational scientist. There is too much risk, too much chance. According to what I have just said, it is quite possible for a specific student to go through a school system, from kindergarten to high school graduation, and get an excellent education because he or she, by chance, was always placed in the right classroom. It is also possible that a student could go that same route and never have a really good teacher.

Each year, I ask more than 100 college seniors why they chose their particular college major (which in many instances is the same as choosing a lifetime profession). More than 90 percent of them give the same answer, "When I was in elementary school [or high school] I had a good teacher in that field." One chance meeting in the schooling process and an entire life has direction. Yes, it is risky; but it is also reality. For the student, the classroom teacher *is* the school system.

For convenience, educators frequently divide the schooling process into three categorical levels: the principle level, the policy level, and the practice level.

During my twenty years in the educational profession, I have seen changes in the principles upon which school officials base decisions. I have seen a greater emphasis on the doctrine of separation of church and state in Supreme Court cases. I have seen restrictions and limitations on school finances. I have seen new attitudes and laws regarding minorities. I have seen changes in course requirements and stiffer teacher-certification standards.

For the crusader who carried the cause, each change in principle represented a major achievement, a worthy accomplishment which followed months, perhaps years, of active battle. Yet, in spite of all those efforts, for most children, school is about the same as it was before the battles were won. If the teacher can relate to the students and has a commitment to teaching, school becomes a delightful place to spend childhood and adolescence.

During my years in teaching, I have also seen changes in educational policies. I have seen the coming and going of dress and hair codes. I have seen the construction and destruction of high school smoking areas. I have seen new emphasis on courses in drugs, economics, values, and driver's education. I have seen an increasing trend to restrict corporal punishment. Yet, school still goes on much as it did 200 years ago.

I have seen changes in educational practices and programs. I have seen the modular schedule come and go. I watched the rise and fall of the open classroom. I have heard the proponents and opponents of individualized instruction, bicultural education, mainstreaming, vocational education, and gifted education. Yet, not all that much has changed.

Despite all the principles, all the policies, and all the programs, the teacher remains the dominant constant in all educational endeavors. Despite all our technology and science, the teaching-learning process is still primarily a human activity. Some highly motivated learners may get some isolated lessons from machines or books, but most of us know most of what we know because someone taught us.

It makes good rhetoric to attack the system, but for the most part the effort is more ambitious than effective. Any real change in the quality of a child's education will begin and be completed not in the United States Congress or in the state capital or in the school board meeting but in the heart and mind of the *individual teacher.*

The System and the Teacher

There is actually an interesting dilemma here because even teachers like to believe in a system. In most cases, the individual teacher is the key to a successful educational experience and to educational progress. The limits to creativity are in the mind of that teacher in that classroom. Yet, a large percentage will argue vehemently that there is indeed a system and that that system prevents them from being as good as they should be. The teachers themselves are the first people who need to understand the guerrilla nature of schools.

When I was a high school principal, we used a standard form for teachers to notify parents if a student was in danger of failing a class. In fact, we required that the forms go out at least four weeks before the final grading if the student was going to receive a failing grade. One day, an algebra teacher came in and asked for sixty forms. Since that represented about 75 percent of his student load, I decided to check into the problem.

He told me, "Yes, they are, in fact, failing algebra."

"But what is the problem? Are they lazy?"

"No," he replied. "They can't do algebra because they can't do simple arithmetic. They can't multiply and divide."

At that particular time in educational history, that report didn't surprise me. Those students had spent their first few years in school during a period of mathematical philosophy which suggested that a child could do calculus before he learned to multiply. Thus, many children didn't learn to multiply. Perhaps the philosophy was sound enough, but those students obviously hadn't learned what that algebra teacher wanted them to know.

However, I thought the solution seemed simple, so I mustered up my fatherly image as best as I could, walked around to his side of my desk in an effort to dethrone myself, took a casual pose, and offered some words of great pedagogical wisdom gathered from decades of varied classroom experience. "Why don't you teach them to multiply?"

"But," he answered too quickly, "if I did that I wouldn't be able to teach algebra."

"Are they learning algebra now?"

"No. Most of them aren't, at least."

"Why not?" This was beginning to sound like a Socratic dialogue with frequent repetitions.

"Because they can't multiply and divide."

"Well, teach them."

"That takes time."

"Sure it does, but what else are you doing with your class time?"

"But I wouldn't get through the book."

"Who says you've got to get through the book?"

"The principal."

I had him there when I realized I was the principal. "No. My recommendation is for you to begin where they are, with work they can do, and proceed from there."

"But," he retorted, as he began walking out the door, "if I did that, I wouldn't be teaching algebra; and that is what I am getting paid to do."

With that, he stormed back to his room and spent the next six months teaching algebra, while I spent those six months trying to explain to parents why their children weren't learning algebra.

That teacher wasn't bitter. He just had a mistaken notion of his task, and he serves as an illustration of the dangers of thinking in terms of a system. In that situation, the system said to teach algebra to freshmen, regardless of individual differences, unique problems, or special needs. The only person who had the power to correct the inaccurate order was the teacher, and he refused to do so. A new policy wouldn't have done much good. A court order wouldn't have changed things that much. Change had to begin in the attitude of that teacher.

The System and the Parent

Don't get me wrong. I know there are some limitations, restrictions, and rules. I have bumped against a few of these myself from time to time. But there are no rules that demand that any teacher be lazy, rude, unimaginative, or ineffective. These are characteristics of teachers and not characteristics of a system.

I visit scores of different school buildings every year. On those visits I see a variety of funny designs and hear about a catalogue of funny rules. But in every building I have ever visited, there are always teachers who are doing a good job of relating to students and are teaching young people the content of effective and efficient living. The individual classroom teacher is still the biggest single issue in determining school excellence in this country.

So we are now back to where we started in this chapter. If you are interested in rallying around noble causes, getting your name in the paper, and winning battles against an anonymous system, you probably won't find much help in this book. But if you are sincerely interested in helping your child survive and perhaps even thrive in this schooling ordeal, and if you are willing to agree that the teacher represents the system to your child, then I think the next three chapters may offer some help and hope. At least, you should know how to tell the difference between Exhibit A and Exhibit C; you should know how some C's became C's; and you should learn what you can do if your child happens to be assigned to a confirmed and card-carrying C. And this is what battling the school "system" is all about.

2

"I'll Just Die If I Don't Get Ms. Brown!"

Choice Time

Briar Common Elementary School is located in a moderately prosperous suburb in any American city. As yet, the district has not had unusual financial problems. There are four sections of the sixth grade at Briar Common, with approximately twenty-five students per section.

The following are sketches of the four sixth-grade teachers. Read the sketches carefully, then respond to the directions which follow.

Mr. Sam Kinner: During the early 1970s when Mr. Kinner worked on his Masters of Teaching degree, he became immersed in the instructional objective approach to teaching, popularized by Mager and Popham. Since then, he has developed a comprehensive, competency-based curriculum, and he uses individualized instruction. For every unit, he has prepared a packet of objectives, readings, and activities. The objectives tell the student exactly what is expected of him. Examples are such things as: "By the end of this unit, the students will be able to construct a friendly letter with no more than three mechanical errors." "By the end of this unit, the student will be able to identify on a map all the countries of South America." The readings provide the necessary information, and the activities specify the practice needed to achieve the objective.

At the beginning of each unit, Mr. Kinner distributes the packets to the students, who then sit at their desks and complete the packets. Some units can be completed in one or two days, but frequently units take as long as a week or more. Mr. Kinner spends most of his time checking student progress, encouraging individuals, and administering progress tests. In his class, efficiency is the key. Since the objectives are clearly written, the students know what they must do. Grades are given fairly and objectively.

Since the students work individually on the packets, desks are arranged to minimize distraction.

Miss Sally Simon: Miss Simon is a fun teacher. She understands children, as well she should because she has had lots of classes in interpersonal relations, communication skills, role playing, and transactional analysis. She believes that students should learn to express themselves, to formulate values, and to think. One of the high spots of each day is the class meeting. During this period the students sit in a circle, and each expresses his or her moods and feelings. This really gets the students ready for the day. It teaches them to be honest with themselves and with others. Some days the class meeting gets so exciting that it might last most of the morning. Miss Simon also believes that students need to be encouraged to be creative, so the class spends a lot of time reading and writing poetry and performing improvisational dramas. Almost any lesson—history, science, math—can be made interesting and relevant.

Most of the time the desks are pushed out of the way, so the students can sit in circles on the floor or can act out their dramas.

Sometimes visitors get the idea that Miss Simon's classes are disorderly and loud, but she explains that by saying students must be active to learn.

If you want to visit, try to come on "pet day." That's when one of the students brings in a pet, and all the students spend the day getting acquainted with that pet. One day a student even brought his boa constrictor.

Mrs. Constance Smith: Last year Mrs. Smith was named District Teacher of the Year. The award was particularly appropriate because she was also celebrating her twenty-fifth year in the district. In fact, she has been a sixth-grade teacher in the same classroom for all those twenty-five years. By now, she and her class are a legend. Students know what to expect when they enroll. To pass Mrs. Smith's class they will have to know the states and capitals, all the presidents in order, the countries of South America, the Books of the Bible (she still insists on this and so far no one has protested), and how to divide and multiply whole numbers and fractions.

In her class the students will diagram sentences, write frequent reports, and work difficult math problems. There will be homework almost every night.

There aren't many distractions in her class. She doesn't like noise, and students quickly learn when to speak and when not to.

The desks are in straight rows. The bulletin boards are really good because Mrs. Smith spends a lot of money for instructional posters and things like that. The chalk board is always clean. The bookcases are neat. If the janitors had a vote, they would make Mrs. Smith District Teacher of the Year every year.

Despite her success and her recognition, Mrs. Smith doesn't seem to be as happy as she used to be.

Mr. Don Huey: Mr. Huey is a busy teacher, and he runs a busy class. During the early 1960s when he did his master's work on a National Science Foundation grant, he committed himself to one educational principle—students must be active. So he keeps them active. He manages this by what he calls the problem-solving method. He gives the students some kind of a problem which demands that they use a wide range of skills and knowledge to solve. This way the day is not divided into blocks of time for arithmetic, history, science, reading, and so on. The students use these skills in solving the problems. Most of the time they work in groups, and frequently they are out of the classroom—in the resource center, on the playground, or even downtown in the museum. Mr. Huey calls himself "a director of learning" rather than a teacher. He spends most of his time discussing progress with one of the groups. When he talks, he uses more interrogative sentences than declarative. He begins sentences with, "Have you considered . . . ?" or "Are you sure . . . ?" or "What do you think . . . ?"

The furniture in the classroom seems disarranged, but it doesn't make much difference. The students never use it anyhow.

Mr. Huey is really a popular teacher, except sometimes with the principal, who thinks Mr. Huey wants to take too many field trips.

Your Test

After you have carefully read each of the four sketches, imagine that you are the parent of an eleven-year-old who is preparing to enter sixth grade at Briar Common Elementary School. Since at Briar Common, parents are given an opportunity to participate, in the educational program, you can help choose your child's teacher.

Based on your present knowledge and philosophy of schools, rank the four teachers according to how you would choose them for your child.

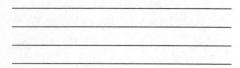

———————————————— Mr. Sam Kinner
———————————————— Miss Sally Simon
———————————————— Mrs. Constance Smith
———————————————— Mr. Don Huey

Now, just for fun, rank the four teachers according to how you would choose them if you were the eleven-year-old student.

_____	Mr. Sam Kinner
_____	Miss Sally Simon
_____	Mrs. Constance Smith
_____	Mr. Don Huey

How did you do on your test? If you found it easy, I commend you. That means that you have strong opinions about the educational process and that you are prepared to handle some of the decisions which are actually being forced upon some parents by legislation and procedure. For example, the new federal, special-education law, Public Law 94-142, requires that parents of special-education students attend and participate in all committee meetings (sometimes called staffings) where an individual child's education is discussed. Since this requirement is receiving favorable reports, it could soon extend to nearly every child in school, and all parents could find themselves making decisions similar to those you just made in this activity.

If you found the test difficult, I commend you. Or, at least, I identify with you. As a parent (even with all my experience in the field of schools), I find the test hard. For one thing, all those teachers are good at what they are doing. There is no clear-cut case of incompetence here as there was in the examples of chapter one. These four persons are dedicated teachers who still believe that children are worth the efforts of hard work, that the system can tolerate inventive teaching, and that schooling makes a difference. This in itself makes Briar Common not so common and the decision not so easy. Here, we are not choosing between good and bad but between a right or wrong approach, and this makes the decision a philosophical one.

If I had used that word, *philosophy,* any earlier, you would have probably lost interest. At least, most people do, but you were actually doing the work of educational philosophy when you ranked those teachers, either from the parent's standpoint or from the student's. The differences among them is not of quality but of philosophy, and you chose one philosophy over another. Of course these four do not exhaust all the possible educational philosophies swarming about, and some of my more theoretical friends in the field would scream about oversimplification. But don't let those screams bother you. You have been philosophizing about education. Those theory-minded people are only making an everyday topic into something difficult.

Sometimes *how* we make decisions is almost as important as the decisions we make. In this case, it is important for you to understand what mental processes and what personal biases you were using when you ranked those teachers.

How Do You Think When You Think About Teachers?

You probably approached the decisions from one of two directions, and the direction you used indicates something about what you think is important to education. The first direction would be the practical approach. If you think this way, you probably said, "I know what I want my children to learn and I know which of these four teachers will get the job done." You might have based your decision on past experience or on the "glorified I"—*I* know how *I* learned and since *I* am almost perfect, everyone else should learn this same way—or you might have based your decision on a feeling of which teacher is most likely to achieve the results you find desirable. All this is practical. You make educational choices based on what works.

The second direction is the more world-viewish one. You might have made your decisions based on such questions as: What is the implied nature of man at work here? In this person's class, what is the basis of knowledge? Who decides what should be learned? What is learning?

Since there is merit in both the practical and the world-view approach, some combination of the two probably offers the best way for us to evaluate these four teachers. We do need to know what kind of immediate results a particular teacher is going to get, but it is also important to know what those results mean and why we want those results for our children. Why do you want your child to score well on standardized tests, to be able to read when he is six, to multiply, to be creative, to have a good self-image?

I really mean those as more than rhetorical questions. I am not asking just to make you think I am profound. I think every thoughtful parent must at some time back away from his child and the immediate situation and ask what all this means. What do you want for your child today? next year? twenty years from now? Based on that, what kind of teacher does your child need? Which of the four is right, not only for your educational expectations, but also for your child's personality and peculiar learning needs?

Actually, the descriptions themselves are a bit deceptive. On the surface, we get a glimpse of what is happening in four different classrooms. But there is more at work here than what is on the surface. In each of those classrooms, there is an educational force at work which is only implied in those descriptions. To understand fully what is happening to your child, you must look beyond the content, the seating arrangement, and the classroom activities to see what is below the surface, below the descriptions.

Hidden Curriculum

In recent years we have been warned: Beware of Hidden Curriculum. The implication of that warning and the warners is that there are some lessons, some very important lessons, hidden within the way we do things as well as what we do. If, these warners say, we are going to make important decisions about education, we must recognize what is being taught *accidentally* as well as intentionally.

Those people may have a point. As adults, we may find that we have strongly developed habits and attitudes that we can't remember learning.

I have always considered myself a nonchauvinistic guy. In fact, at times I have been rather persuasive in convincing high school females that they should be doctors instead of nurses and lawyers instead of secretaries. I am proud of my record. Yet, the other day I drove into a gas station, and a young lady came out to service my car. Well, I'm not *that* liberal. There are still some things which are sacred to masculinity, and my car is one of them. Not only did I not trust my machine to that female mind, but I was also embarrassed to stand there and let this girl do men's work. I cowered on the other side of the auto, walked around as if I were a stranger there, read all the labels in the pop machine, and hid in the men's room for about ten minutes.

Now, I am confused. I don't know how to handle my attitudes toward male supremacy. I have consciously and rationally dealt with the major issues, and I had made a rational decision. But I have discovered that somewhere in my past, completely without my will and without my knowledge, I have learned (yes, *learned*) some very strong attitudes toward sex roles. When did that creep in? I don't know. I never had a lesson in it. I never read a book or saw a film about it. But somewhere I have learned never to trust cars to women. (As the commercial says, "You can trust your car to the *man*. . . .")

That is the hidden curriculum. In his book, *The Abolition of Man,* C. S. Lewis talks about a rather innocent-looking grammar text. Yet, the approach the authors take toward language is not grammar but ethics, philosophy; and Lewis makes the point that ten years hence, the students will take a side in an argument without ever realizing how they developed their position. Not only is there such a thing as a hidden curriculum, but it deserves our attention.

Everything the teacher does in the classroom teaches your child something. Every book your child reads teaches him something, both in bold print and between the lines. Every television program, every statement and action you make, every newspaper story your child reads—all blend together and have some effect in shaping that wonderful and mysteriously beautiful thing called your child's mind.

The purpose of this chapter is to help you detect and evaluate the hidden curriculum inherent in a teacher's approach to teaching; but rather than doing the work of investigation for you, I am going to dwell on the technique—to provide you with a method of investigation. Then, if you ever have to make real decisions similar to those you made at the beginning of the chapter, you will have a framework from which to operate. And even if you are not asked to choose which teacher your child has, you will at least be able to understand and help him deal with the hidden lessons he is receiving.

So with that, let's look at the four teachers. Although each represents a certain philosophical school which comes complete with a polysyllabic title, the labels are generalizations which might get in the way of real investigation, so we will ignore those. Besides, if you used the labels, your friends would think you were doing the work of educational philosophy and would lose all confidence in you.

Kinner: Mr. Kinner does not define education as the process of socialization. That is probably the most distinguishing thing about him. For centuries, some of the other educators have claimed that the value of schools is to teach children how to be social beings, how to get along with their peers, and then how to get along in society when school is finished.

I don't mean to imply that there is no socialization in Mr. Kinner's class, but it is not the key lesson, the real issue. For him, the real purpose of schools is to master the written material. The lessons are on paper, not within people. A child's task is to take this written material, study it, and bring it back to the conscious level when it is demanded.

If you look deeply enough into this, you will get an ever-so-small hint that a child and a dog are different only in the child's ability to read. You could use the same principles to train the dog. Decide what you want him to do, create the training sessions with repetition and feedback, and give him a biscuit when he performs. In fact, some of the granddaddies of this kind of teaching make that point loudly, but maybe posterity has improved the procedure.

Of course, reading is absolutely essential in this classroom. If the student doesn't know how to read well, he probably won't like the class very much and he won't do well. (That is the first human principle a teacher must know: We enjoy doing what we do well. Conversely, we don't like doing what is hard for us.) Perhaps Mr. Kinner will make some provisions for his slower readers, but the emphasis is still there. Those students who read quickly will finish faster, so they will probably be encouraged to do more work. But the slower readers will struggle to cover the minimum.

There is an interesting formula within this emphasis on the printed word.

Reading = studying

Studying = learning

Therefore:

Reading = learning

If you want to make a big deal of your philosophical work, you can tell your friends that you have just completed an Aristotelian syllogism.

The question is not whether the formula is true some of the time. Surely it is. But the question is whether it is true all the time. Is reading the only way for you or your child to learn something?

Students in Mr. Kinner's class will need to be self-motivated. If they are not interested in learning this material, they could easily whittle every cumulus cloud in the sky into dragons and serpents and *Star Wars* characters, and rarely get to the task. Of course, Mr. Kinner has built in some rewards for those who complete their work, but those rewards must be more valuable than mentally whittled cloud dragons if they are going to be of much use.

Some students are particularly well-suited for this class. They are people whose psychological makeup demands organization and direction. They do their best work when the route is clearly defined. These people would function well here because there is direction and little interference.

Of the four teachers discussed, Mr. Kinner would probably do the best job of preparing students to excel on standardized tests. So, if your educational goal for your child is a good score on the SAT or ACT tests, then you would have done well if you chose Mr. Kinner.

Simon: Miss Simon is almost the opposite of Mr. Kinner. He is organized; she is disorganized. He knows where he is going; she lets direction come with the moment. He puts emphasis on the written word; she emphasizes the people. He is interested in acquiring information; she is interested in watching the inner self unfold.

In an effort to understand students better, educators have recently used the tool of dividing the human into three parts or domains: 1. the cognitive domain—the area of factual data and concepts built off those facts; 2. the affective domain—the area of emotions, values, and feelings; and 3. the psychomotor domain—the area of physical movement.

In this division, Mr. Kinner deals almost exclusively in the cognitive and Miss Simon deals almost exclusively in the affective.

Miss Simon puts a high worth on the value of the human being.

The individual is almost a sacred thing to her. Although she has a social classroom, the individual student is not forced into conformity. He is, on the other hand, encouraged to discover himself.

If you are one of those people who have criticized the schooling process for being a leveling monster which tries to make all the people the same or you criticize because school squelches the creativity out of children, then Miss Simon is your choice.

Smith: Mrs. Smith is an interesting alternative to the first two. Like Mr. Kinner, she deals in the cognitive, but she does encourage socialization. The students at least will interact with her, or listen to her as she speaks to the class.

The thing that is really important in Mrs. Smith's class is Mrs. Smith—not the lesson and not the children. She has the children where they can see her. The bulletin board represents her work. She makes the decisions about what is to be learned.

But this is not all bad. A benevolent dictatorship may be the kindest form of government, particularly in a classroom where someone has to make some decisions.

As a traditional teacher, Mrs. Smith is interested in perpetuating the status quo. She is interested in preparing your child to live in society, not change it or fight against it.

If you believe that there are certain essentials which every human being must learn in order to survive his native land, and if you want those essentials taught to your child in a no-nonsense but caring way, Mrs. Smith is your choice.

Although it won't make much difference in the way she treats your child, it is correct that Mrs. Smith isn't as happy as she used to be. It has become rather difficult to be an enthusiastic traditionalist in today's schools. Even if you picked her first, you are not as sure about the decision as your parents would have been. In order for Mrs. Smith to function, she must have support—support from an administration which has probably read tons of books about educational innovation and nifty teaching methods and support from parents, like yourself, who will listen to children read, turn off the television after supper, supervise arithmetic lessons, and read the notes pinned to the child's shirt when he gets home in the afternoon. She is just not getting the kind of support she used to. And the other teachers probably snicker behind her back.

Huey: Mr. Huey doesn't like Mrs. Smith; that's for sure. Or at least, he doesn't like her teaching methods. In fact, he probably entered teaching to counteract the work of all the "Mrs. Smiths" in the world. He had some himself, probably learned more than he thought he did, but decided there was a better way to teach.

Like Miss Simon, Mr. Huey emphasizes the person. But where Miss Simon relies on experience, raw native experience, as a teaching vehicle, he takes the enterprise further. He wants the students to have real experiences, but he wants them to run their experiences through their rational thinking processes. He may turn the students loose with that boa constrictor; but when the playing is over, he will ask some rather difficult questions. "Why did the snake skin feel bony? Why were his eyes so dim?" Those are different questions from Miss Simon's, "How did the snake feel? Did you enjoy holding it?"

Mr. Huey believes in teaching the material, but for him the material is anything that relates to the child's particular problem at that particular time. You may want to ask, "When will my child learn to divide fractions?" Mr. Huey will answer, "When he needs to." And that is his definition of learning. For him, learning goes beyond memorizing facts or studying books. (Remember the formula—whoops, syllogism—we worked out with Mr. Kinner?) Learning is applying the facts to the problem at hand. Mr. Huey won't force a child to learn anything until he has a need for it, but he *will* help to create a need.

Mr. Huey also emphasizes socialization. These students learn in groups. They are expected to help each other and learn from each other. This is what he calls "teaching the democratic process," solving real problems in groups.

There is a kind of deceptiveness in his popularity though. A few years ago researchers surveyed the attitudes of seventh graders concerning school. They found that the happiest seventh graders in the nation were in classrooms more like Mrs. Smith's than Mr. Huey's. Oh well, what does research prove?

A Personal Test

After reading the discussion, are you still satisfied with your choice, or have you changed your mind? There isn't any penalty for being indecisive while you are reading this book, but I do hope you are prepared to make a definite decision should you ever be confronted with the choice.

If you are still having trouble deciding which philosophy you prefer or even deciding what difference it makes, here are a few illustrations of typical experiences which you may encounter as a parent. Your choice of one course of action over another demonstrates your own personal philosophy of child rearing. This, in turn, should help you decide what kind of teacher your child needs.

1. Let's suppose you have a youngster at your house who is at that precious age when he is just beginning to walk. You remember the age. The child is clumsy, but inquisitive. At times, his energy level is almost unbearable. He is constantly moving, pulling, checking, banging. By himself, he creates as much activity as a house full of kittens.

Now, here is the problem. How do you handle the child's development at this stage? Do you put all your good stuff away and let the child roam around at will—investigating and breaking and checking and botching? Or do you, on the other hand, leave the good stuff out and teach that child the meaning of the word *no?*

These are really the only two options. You may want to propose a compromise like putting away the good stuff and still teaching him to leave things alone, but that is avoiding the issue. The emphasis is still on your teaching the child to restrict his natural impulses and to get in line with social behavior. You just don't have as much confidence in your ability as a teacher as I originally proposed.

So without compromise, which is the appropriate course of action? How you answer that question reveals a great deal about your philosophical position, and it does relate you to one of the four teachers.

For example, Miss Simon would argue that a child should never be restricted at this age. If your good stuff is that precious to you, put it away, but don't limit the child's curiosity and creativity. She would contend that letting the child get in touch with what is inside him is more important than what society demands.

Mr. Huey would probably agree with Miss Simon in part, but he would make more of the opportunity. He would try to turn the child's activities into something productive.

On the other hand, Mrs. Smith would get right to the issue. Children must learn to get along in society. They must learn that there are restrictions and limitations, that natural impulses are not always right and must be curtailed. She would leave the good things out and spank the child's grubby hands until he has learned those lessons.

Mr. Kinner would begin with the same principle as Mrs. Smith, but he would use a different technique. He would probably manufacture some kind of a reward system for when the child did leave things alone, and he would rely on his rewards more than on punishment.

For any parent, this is a real situation. Here philosophy is applied; theory becomes practice. What you do reveals your beliefs more clearly than any pronouncement you could ever make. You are an educational philosopher, whether you want to be one or not. Let's try another test.

2. Although it's not very cold, you have just had ten inches of snow, and the superintendent called off school for the day. Would you rather have your child sitting in front of the fireplace reading a book or out in the yard building a snowman? Again, these are the only two options. Don't make the test more complex than it is.

By now you should be getting a feel for the four philosophies and should be able to anticipate how the teachers would respond. Mr. Huey and Miss Simon both believe in direct experience over the more mediated experience of reading. Mr. Huey, particularly, is not opposed to reading, but he wouldn't want the child to lose the opportunity of having this wonderful snow for a teacher. Miss Simon would choose the snow anytime.

Mrs. Smith would not be opposed to a brief romp in the snow as a break, but she is more excited about children who are "turned on to reading" or who have discovered that "reading is FUNdamental." She would not want the child to waste all of this fine opportunity without reading something.

Mr. Kinner would probably favor the reading too, but he would give the child enough hot chocolate to keep him interested and quiet.

3. This test is primarily for fathers, but mothers can play too. Your son has just turned seventeen, has completed the high school driver's education course with flying colors, and has decorated his wallet with the most precious piece of paper of any American adolescent—the driver's license.

For years he has prepared for this moment. He has saved his money from lawn mowing, the paper route, and the part-time job; and now he wants wheels of his own. Cautiously, you give in, and the search for the "magic pumpkin" begins. Finally, one day he calls you. After days of diligent searching, he has found the char-iot of his dreams—the finest vehicle on earth—and he is bringing it home for your blessing before the marriage is consummated.

Well, when he drives up, you know you're in trouble, and one brief walk around the car confirms your suspicions. You see all the evidences of past abuse and imminent heartache—the worn tires, the sagging shocks, the collected crud in the exhaust pipe. But you also see the gleam in your son's eyes. And perhaps you even remember some dream you once had.

What do you do? Do you exercise the prerogative of experience and forbid this purchase outright? Do you attempt to use logic and reason, knowing both will have little impact? Or do you say, "What's the use? He will only learn from experience," and gra-ciously offer your blessing?

Remember our four teachers and try to think what each would do if, as a parent, he could be true to his philosophy. Again, Mr. Huey and Miss Simon believe in the value of experience. The only way for your son to learn is to let him get involved. But Mrs. Smith and Mr. Kinner both believe that as an adult you have the obligation to prevent his suffering and financial loss.

4. Finally, we get to the big test. And this one is real for every parent. It is a simple but universal question. When do you teach your child the facts of life? Notice that I am inferring here that this is the responsibility of the parent and not of the school. In following chapters, I will defend that contention. For the sake of this illustration, please assume that I am accurate.

There are two schools of thought here. One says that you wait until the child comes to you with questions; then you answer only the questions he or she asks. The other school says that if you wait it is too late. You must choose the proper time, bring the child to you, and fill the young mind with all the information he or she is going to need to know when the opportunities and de-sires become more real than they are at the present time.

Let me emphasize that it doesn't take any imagination to make up a situation like this. This is a real problem. Every parent faces it, and you must choose one of those two positions. Do you believe, as Mr. Huey would, that children only learn what they are interested in—that there is no value in storing information in the mind in hopes it might be used later? Or do you believe, as Mrs. Smith would, that you can teach your child lessons that he will remember when he needs to remember them?

Although you may never have to write the answers to the above questions on a test, and you may never have to verbalize your thinking, you *are* going to take a philosophical stand on the issues whether you want to or not. Some parents think they have avoided the question of when to tell the child the facts of life by ignoring the issue completely; but that, too, is a philosophical position. I suggest that you will come closer to getting it right if you have thought about it beforehand.

This is the conclusion of our test. Let me assure you that I have not forgotten the original purpose of this chapter, which is to help you understand the philosophical implications of various teaching procedures. The purpose of the test is to help you identify what hidden meaning your actions have so that you can understand more clearly what a specific teacher is doing.

Now that you are in touch with your own thoughts and you have some idea of what you think is best for your child, let me summarize with a checklist that should help you identify the philosophical implications of a specific classroom. Remember, we are not dealing here with good and bad. In succeeding chapters I will speak specifically about how to evaluate teachers' performances, whether good or bad. But here, I am only interested in your being able to analyze a particular philosophical approach. I do not wish to pass judgment on any one of these four teachers. Although I personally prefer one approach over another, I would prefer any one of the four over Exhibit C in chapter one.

The Checklist

1. *Room Arrangement.* The arrangement of furniture in a room provides a great deal of information about the teacher. Are the desks arranged so that the students can relate to each other? Where has the teacher placed his or her desk, the symbol of authority in the classroom? Are the desks arranged in such a way as to provide ample opportunity for discussion? Is the room arrangement permanent or flexible?

2. *Room Decoration.* Most teachers believe that physical appearance of the classroom is a part of the instructional process so they work at decorating the room to reflect their teaching suppositions. You can make some rather valid assumptions about the teacher just by studying those decorations. Is the room decorated with student-produced material or is it decorated with more professional material? If student material is used, is it material that was produced just to decorate the bulletin boards or was it assigned as a part of a larger instructional objective? Are the books in the bookcase arranged neatly? Is the teacher's desk organized or cluttered? (Although I have only observations and no statistics to prove my point, I am convinced that there is a definite correlation between neatness and noise level. Students are quieter when the books are orderly and the teacher's desk top is visible through the papers.)

Are the bulletin boards current? Are they there for instructional purposes or decoration? And above all, if the room is decorated with student material, is the teacher proud of it? Does she call your attention to it? Occasionally I enter a classroom as a casual visitor, knowing the venture will consume at least half an hour. Some teachers demand that every visitor see everything the students have done. I like these people. If I were in the sixth grade, I would like to be in their classes because they like children and children's ideas.

3. *Teaching Activities.* Check with your child or other children in the classroom to determine what kinds of activities are prominent. Usually from conversations with students you can tell how much time is allotted to discussion, direct teacher talk, individual work, films, field trips, fair projects, and other activities.

4. *The Role of the Textbook.* As one more measure, check to see if you can determine how dependent the teacher is on the textbook. Teachers who rely heavily on textbooks are usually people who believe that education is a process of cultural transmission. They have content to cover, and the book offers an efficient, organized way to get to it.

Summary:

Let me emphasize again that the preceding checklist is not a test of quality but a test to determine underlying presuppositions. Of course, the list is incomplete, but it should provide you with enough evidence to make a rather valid assumption about the philosophical position of a specific teacher.

Obviously, no teacher is going to be a pure representative of a particular position. I intentionally drew those illustrations at the beginning with strong distinguishing characteristics. Most teachers are some synthesis of all four, depending on situations and students. So don't be shocked if a "Mrs. Smith" sometimes acts like a "Mr. Huey." But I do think you can find trends which reflect presuppositions; and now that you are an educational philosopher, you are in a better position to decide what is best for your child. Once that is established, you can begin to work on the problem of teaching quality, the subject of chapter three.

3

"Some of 'Em Teach Us Real Good!"

Like any other theory, educational theory isn't much good until it is put into practice. Any idea, any presupposition, any great-sounding philosophy must eventually stand the test of the classroom. A teacher's profound recitations of the doctrines of a Plato or a John Dewey don't mean much to your child in the midst of a long-division lesson. Having a philosophy is important to the teacher and eventually to the student, but it doesn't do much good if the teacher doesn't have the enthusiasm, compassion, and intelligence to bring it to life in the classroom.

As a parent, you need to be able to distinguish between the Smiths and Kinners; but you also need to know how to distinguish between good and bad teaching. The first part of this chapter focuses on that problem. The second part offers some suggestions for what to do if your child happens to be assigned to a teacher whose incompetence overshadows his presuppositions. The third part attempts to explain why some good teachers turn sour.

Teaching is a human profession and, as such, it has its flaws and weaknesses. Regardless of how good a particular system may be, there are always a few poor pedagogical practices. The professional teachers don't endorse these, nor do the administrators; yet, they creep in. Sometimes only the students (and their parents if there are adequate communication channels) are even aware of the bad classroom procedure. Generally, students are powerless to correct these; so if there is to be any improvement, the parents will have to assume some responsibility. The Christian parent, because of his interest in justice and because of his skill in human relations, is a desirable candidate to initiate positive action.

But while discovering any teaching weaknesses you really shouldn't make a nuisance of yourself. So to simplify your task, I submit the following list of characteristics of good teachers. I warn you that the list reflects my bias, but it is based on several years of observation. The list is to be taken as a whole. A teacher's violation of one of these points does not necessarily condemn him or her to the pedagogical junkyard, but these are points to investigate. If too many are absent, you may have a legitimate problem.

1. Good Teachers Read and Hand Back Homework Assignments. Make a point to check your child's homework assignment each day and ask to look at it when it is returned. If it isn't returned, you probably should start getting concerned.

Some college students who have suspected that their fine writings were going unread have inserted into their papers such sentences as *Underline this sentence if you are still reading at this point.* They then spread the results of the investigation around campus.

I don't really recommend deliberate traps, but the point is clear enough. If the work is valuable enough to justify the child's doing it, it is valuable enough to merit the teacher's reading.

And this leads us to the second characteristic.

2. Good Teachers Give Worthwhile Assignments. It's confession time. On rare occasions, I have been known to give a homework assignment, maybe even a big one, just to keep the students busy on something. I realize no other teacher in the world is that lazy, but I offer this characteristic just in case your child should ever be in my class.

A child's time is precious. There are too many things to learn and too little time to learn them. Teachers really shouldn't waste children's time on busywork. Look at your child's homework to see whether the lessons to be learned justify the amount of time it takes him to complete the assignment.

Let me clarify this with an example. A few years ago, I asked a rather intelligent, high school junior to help me after school one evening. He couldn't. He had a long, English grammar assignment. I can empathize, so I suggested that perhaps I could help.

He said that I couldn't; it was something he had to do himself. But I persisted until he showed it to me. The teacher's objective was to refresh these active, busy, high school juniors on the use of commas. The assignment was for them to copy ninety-six long sentences from a textbook and place commas in the appropriate place—let me repeat—copy *word for word* ninety-six sentences from a text and place commas where they belonged.

I can understand teaching commas. I can even understand asking some students who are having trouble with their writing to copy sentences word for word. But this teacher was dishonest with those students. If they didn't need to copy sentences, and I suspect they didn't, she should have typed the sentences herself and handed them to the students. This was a busywork assignment which grew out of a teacher's laziness.

3. *Good Teachers Stay in the Classroom.* The best way to check this is to listen to your child's stories. If he has too many tales of eraser fights and classroom chaos, the teacher is probably having coffee problems.

4. *Good Teachers Decorate Their Rooms.* This repeats the observations of the previous chapter, so I won't go into more detail.

5. *Good Teachers Are Organized.* Good teachers know where they are going. Students in their classes know where they are going. If your child seems to be having difficulty in determining direction or what is expected of him, the teacher may not be preparing sufficiently.

Actually, poor preparation is the cause of many classroom problems. When young teachers come to me and ask for help with classroom discipline, I first ask to see their lesson plans. When a teacher has stayed up late in the night to plan an exciting and valuable lesson, he will probably demand the right to teach that lesson. Your child and every other student will profit.

6. *Good Teachers Communicate with Parents.* Teachers complain about not getting parental support, but some teachers forget to ask for it. If you discover that you are not being told about problems or that you are being told too late, you may want to investigate the teacher's energy level.

7. *Good Teachers Don't Lose Control of Themselves.* Teaching is a disease that attacks the nervous system first. Interacting with twenty-five defiant youngsters is not a particularly pleasant way to spend an afternoon. Sometimes a teacher reaches his breaking point. I have full sympathy for such a person, and I understand how that can happen. But it can't be tolerated. Teachers cannot respond to misbehavior with anger, maliciousness, or violence. The teacher must control the situation; but he has no right to ridicule, strike in anger, or abuse a student. There is no room in the profession for teachers who react this way.

8. *Good Teachers Don't Lose Control of the Classroom.* For the last ten years the Gallup Poll, as published each fall in the *Phi Delta Kappan* magazine, has indicated that lack of discipline is considered the number one problem in American schools. Lack of discipline *is* a problem. Rowdiness and destruction are rampant. Schools have initiated a plethora of sociologically and psychologically sound programs in an attempt to restore order. But programs fail when there are no people to carry them out.

The individual classroom teacher is the key to order. (If this is beginning to sound redundant, remember that "repetition is the mother of studies" and that this is a book about education.)

There is no one technique or one surefire method for establishing control, but good teachers are in control. Of course, being in control needs some interpretation. Not all silent classes are in control, and not all noisy ones are out of control. A teacher is in control when the students are responding to her direction and objectives for the class. Check to see if your child is learning or wasting time.

9. *Good Teachers Give Students a Sense That the Material Is Important.* Educators talk about motivation, but most of us don't even know what the animal looks like; but if your child rushes home with a burning desire to get at his homework and do it just as Mrs. Doe suggested, Mrs. Doe is probably a fairly good teacher.

10. *Good Teachers Don't Abuse Their Right to Academic Freedom.* I am a strong supporter of academic freedom, particularly when I can define what it is; but a teacher does not have a right to offend a child. By law, teachers can't teach religion in public schools; but by the same law, they can't ridicule it either. We need to realize that some of those Supreme Court cases protect the Christian as well as limit him. Teachers cannot use the classroom for a showcase of their personal beliefs, values, or life-styles.

As a member of the human race, a teacher has every right to be what he is. But he cannot use his position of authority to persuade, and he cannot present opinion as fact.

Of course, most of this is subtle, but some of it is downright blatant.

Each year I go to one of the local high schools and lecture to the seniors. The purpose is purely methodological. The teacher wants to train the students in listening and taking notes, skills which are vital to college success. (And I might add that I am a good choice for this role. My lectures are so disorganized and dull that I can prepare those students for anything.)

Since the object is method instead of content, I get to pick the topic. Last spring, I talked about the history of first century Rome—a thrilling subject, relevant to dynamic seventeen-year-olds. However, I did warn them at the beginning that I was going to interject personal opinion and half-truth into the data. I challenged them to sort through this and demand proof. After talking loud and fast for about forty-five minutes, I gave a short quiz. One of the questions was, "True or False: Rome fell because it did not have a workable program of planned obsolescence."

Now, look at that question. It is as loaded as a missile silo. It is a question of economic theory presented as a question of economic fact. Regardless of how he responds, the student has endorsed an opinion, and his "objective" grade will be based on the opinion he endorses.

This question is illegal. This procedure is illegal. Teachers *cannot* teach this way.

Fortunately, most students wrote "Unfair question" and refused to answer. Unfortunately, a few students answered the question without reservation. What would your senior have done?

Facing the Problem

Just reading this list isn't going to make you an expert on teacher evaluation, and I probably should remind you of the old adage, "A little learning is a dangerous thing." The educational scientists themselves have difficulty agreeing on the difference between good and bad teaching, but you should at least have some idea as to what your child's comments reveal about his teacher. I would recommend that you not be too alarmed by stories of isolated incidents similar to some in the above list, but if you begin to detect a frequency or a trend, you may need to exercise your right as a taxpayer and an educator. You may need to become an educational quality-control consultant. You may need to visit the schools.

When that time comes, however, it is important for you to do it right. If you make the wrong moves here, not only could you be ineffective, you might even be damaging. So I offer the following list of rules. Again, these rules are tempered from a teacher's point of view. I do want you to be heard; I do want the situation to be corrected; but I think I understand how to speak to teachers in a way that gets the best results.

The Rules

1. Don't Yell "Wolf!" If you shout too much about every little thing, you will soon develop laryngitis and no one will hear you. Reserve your school visits for significant injustices. If you are fortunate, you may never have to go.

2. Get All the Facts. I would never imply that your child might lie, but some do. It is a rather natural human act, in fact. Sometimes children get so involved in telling a story that they lose sight of the boundary between fact and fiction. And perceptions themselves are sometimes distorted in the heat of the moment. The big boys might not have really set fire to the paper in the bathroom. The teacher may not be as rude as he seems to a fourth grader. These do make interesting stories and everything your child tells you merits your attention, but just make sure you have both sides of the situation.

3. Try To Understand the Problem from the Teacher's Point of View. There may be extenuating circumstances that must be considered. A few years ago, I met a teacher who had been highly recommended, by both his former and present students. Yet, I found him negative, abrupt, and abrasive. I decided the students had overrated him. Later, I learned that his wife had died about a month before our first meeting. The students knew this and they were willing to allow him time to mourn his loss. Can we do less?

4. Go Straight to the Source. If the teacher is inadequate, he is the one to whom you need to address the problem. Go to him first. If he doesn't respond, go through the appropriate chain of command. But start with the teacher.

5. Don't Put the Teacher on the Defensive. Don't go if you are angry.

6. Don't Be Afraid to Compliment a Teacher. You are then in a better position to take issue with him later. A brief note of appreciation for some specific lesson or act can go a long way in making a teacher happier with his salary, and paper isn't all that expensive. Besides he will get the idea that you have good judgment.

7. Don't Make the Teacher Feel Worse Than He Already Does. If you go visit a teacher for something he has done in a fit of passion, don't be surprised to find him already remorseful. In that case, he needs your friendship, not your sharp tongue. Good teachers sometimes make mistakes, but they are aware of them. They don't need you to point them out.

8. *Always Approach a Teacher with the Purpose of Correction.*   If the situation gets so bad that you feel you have to make your appearance, don't go with the idea that you are going to get someone fired. That isn't scriptural. Part of the gospel, the good news of our Savior, is that people can change. As a Christian, your only purpose can be to hope to correct the situation, to make things better for the children in the classroom. And it might not hurt for you to believe in the teacher's ability to improve.

9. *Remember Individual Differences.*   Because of the nature of classrooms, teachers must teach to the norm, the average. If your child doesn't fit into that norm, then that is your problem. He will need your patience and your supplementary help. Don't label a teacher as bad simply because he or she is not reaching one child.

Don't forget that there are children at both ends of the norm. Your child may need special attention in a specific skill because he has a different learning style. Your child may also need special attention because he learns faster than the normal child. Frequently, the results are similar for both extremes. The faster child becomes bored with the pace. He develops habits of carelessness. Those habits grow stronger, and soon the child is behind. He begins to make poor grades. He becomes a behavior problem.

Good teachers know these things and see them developing. But unfortunately, when a teacher has thirty unique human creations in a classroom, she simply can't anticipate and correct every tendency.

The first step in your becoming an educational asset to your child is to become objective about his uniqueness. If you need help understanding this, visit the teacher. She probably has analyzed the situation.

10. *Don't Sue.*   Look! I'm a taxpayer too. To sue the public school is to sue yourself. If you have a point to prove, there are

cheaper ways to go about it. Check to see how much legal fees
have increased in your district's budget during the past five years.

The Step Beyond: Understanding

Now that you are skilled at detecting poor teaching and you
have some idea of how to help your child through a siege of weak
pedagogy, let me suggest one more humanitarian investigation. I
think you, your child, and the teaching profession could profit
from your spending a few minutes wondering why there are weak
teachers in the first place.

I doubt that there is a weak teacher anywhere who once said
during his college days, "I think I'll be a teacher and I think I will
be bad at it." Every year I teach scores of college seniors who plan
to enter the field. Every one of those bright, eager, young people
intends to be good. I have never had one who planned to be bad.

So we know that weak teaching is not a result of intention.
Sometimes young teachers are not as good as they should be because they lack experience and adequate preparation. If they survive the first few years without permanently damaging young
lives and the American society, they could become good teachers.

On the other hand, frequently teachers start out with a burst of
enthusiasm, creativity, and effectiveness and through the years
deteriorate into weak, bland, disinterested teachers. These latter
people don't seem to improve with experience. They just continue
to stay in the classroom, be Exhibit C's of the first chapter, and
dream of retirement in some village which is off limits to anyone
below twenty-one.

Those teachers who lose their enthusiasm and effectiveness
over a period of years present a major problem to the quality of
American education. (All the journals and newspapers refer to
this as "teacher burn-out," but I am trying to avoid clichés, so I
won't use that term.) I don't have some magic solution for re-

versing the trend, nor do I have much advice for helping renew any specific teacher; but I would like to offer some reasons for this problem occurring. Again, these reasons are from a teacher's point of view, but that view may help you understand some of the pressures which will eventually affect your child's education.

1. Teaching Is a Continuous-Pressure Job. I hear those comments about the long vacations and short days, but teaching is still a pressure activity. A shoe salesman may stay at the store a little longer than a teacher stays at school, but when the salesman goes home at night, he probably realizes he is finished for the day. There is nothing he can do during that time at home to make himself a more effective shoe salesman. On the other hand, a teacher, especially a good teacher, has very few evenings in his life when he is free from the tyranny of tomorrow's lesson. Regardless of how prepared he may be, he can always prepare some more. There is always another book on the subject which he has never read. There is always a school activity where his students are demonstrating their talents. There are papers to be read, records to keep, plans to be made—for a good teacher, the day never ends. He just decides he must quit. In the past twenty years, I have never gone to bed feeling that I have finished for the day. Some teachers may not always respond to the pressure, but just knowing it is there will eventually make one weary.

2. Good Teaching Doesn't Have Many Immediate Results. Regardless of what surface reasons teachers use for getting into the profession, most of us had, somewhere in the bottoms of our minds, some idea that we were going to make the world better. And we may be doing that, but it will be at least twenty years before we know. In the meantime, we busy ourselves with earth-shaking issues such as the difference between a B and a C grade, gum chewing versus no gum chewing, and the five reasons for

the French Revolution. While teachers are doing this year after
year, parents watch their children grow through the impetuous-
ness of childhood, the awkwardness of early adolescence, the
seriousness of later adolescence, the experimentation of early
adulthood, and the fulfillment of life. If your child makes it
through all these stages and turns out all right, you are going to
rejoice in it, but that fourth-grade teacher will still be collecting
milk money and wondering about the meaning of life.

3. *Teachers Don't Get Paid Much.* (And I promised not to use
clichés). I am not trying to solicit sympathy, but this is a fact of
life. Teachers' salaries are actually relative, according to the local
standard of living. In some places salaries are sufficient to permit
the teacher to enjoy a standard of living equal to most of the other
people in the community. If this is so, teachers don't really deserve sympathy. But in many affluent communities, salaries will
not permit teachers the same standard of living. Again, I don't
feel sorry for the teacher. He knew what the salary scale was
when he entered the profession. But this lower standard of living
also means that the teacher's family must sacrifice because the
wage earner chose that profession. At this point in his life, a
teacher-parent may get grumpy when he must continuously tell
his own children that they can't keep up with the kids down the
block.

4. *Teaching Is an Extension of One's Personality.* I have tried to
lay bricks, and I am terrible at it. I can't scoop up the proper
amount of mortar; I can't keep the seams straight; and I have absolutely no sense of plumb. I simply don't have the skill to lay
bricks. You could tell me that, and it wouldn't bother me much.
It's only a skill.

But teaching is more than a skill. Teaching is something that
involves my personality, my very personhood. If you tell me that

I am not a good teacher, you have not merely assessed a skill, you have attacked me as a person. I am sure most people have a sense of pride about their work. None of us likes to be told that we are not good at what we do. But because teaching requires so much ego involvement, teachers are very vulnerable to criticism. I have known some rather competent teachers who have been almost destroyed by critical remarks made by their superiors, their students, or parents of their students. Listening to those kinds of remarks too long will make even the strong become defensive, paranoid, or apathetic.

The Consequences of Understanding

I have not offered the above list to solicit your sympathy, nor do I propose that you rush out and start some charitable cause for old, worn-out teachers. I simply want to introduce you to the pressures which thoughtful, caring, giving teachers face. Of course, everyone faces pressures in his work, and, there are certainly pressures in being a parent. We can't escape these, and I don't really want to make teachers into a special case. But if in your mission to help your child survive and thrive you ever have to confront bad teaching, you need to have some understanding of those pressures unique to teachers. Without that understanding, there will be no effective communication, and without effective communication there will be no positive change.

I also intend for the above list to lead us to a reassuring conclusion to this sometimes negative chapter. Teachers are human. As such they have weaknesses and they make mistakes. Parents who are interested in their child's education must be alert to the possibility of incompetence and error. But most teachers are actually rather nice people. Your child's teacher may not be getting the job done. He may be making some noticeable mistakes. But despite all that, he is probably a pretty decent sort. In all my asso-

4

"I Know All About Morality and Emotions—We Studied That Stuff for Almost a Week in English Class."

In the first three chapters of this section, I have concentrated on the individual classroom teacher. For a given child, this is the appropriate focus. Good teachers can turn almost any program into great educational experiences, while weak teachers will always yield unsatisfactory results regardless of the quality of the program or the architecture.

However, in this concluding chapter, I want to broaden the perspective by including a discussion of the school system itself. Here I would like to focus on some of the problems which are currently perplexing educators, complicating the purpose of schools, and affecting educational quality.

Developing a long list enumerating all these problems is an entertaining way to spend a rainy Saturday afternoon, but it isn't all that profitable. The lists are so common that it would be difficult to add something new. However, if one is to be involved with the schools, he must be acutely aware of these problems. So rather than list them, I will discuss only two—the school's role as a social healer and the deteriorating family—and I will let these serve as examples.

The School as a Social Healer

In contemporary American society, schools have been given the primary responsibility for doctoring every social disease we encounter. When drug abuse duped our adolescents and young adults, the schools were mandated by law to correct the problem with something in the curriculum called drug education. When our young people were seduced into free love, venereal disease, and unwanted pregnancies, the schools implemented a program of correction with another ambiguous pill called sex education. When people began to wreck their lives in automobile accidents, the schools proposed to correct the situation with driver's education. When middle-aged America became fat and flabby and susceptible to early heart attacks, state lawmakers solved the problem by making physical education compulsory for children.

And the beat goes on. Some of the offerings around the nation include courses in such things as death and dying, values, responsibility, consumer knowledge, capitalism, race problems, and hygiene.

This is what some educators have called the "add-a-course mentality." It makes no difference what the problem is or how elusive its solution, the school can just add a course as an instant cure. But it is not as easy as it sounds.

Quite frequently, the professional educators have had the responsibility of correction mandated to them by law, not by choice; and they don't know how to handle it. The idea that anything can be made into a course of study is wrong. Educators have done the best they can. They know that a course contains goals, a body of knowledge, text materials, and some kind of an objective evaluation system. So they apply those criteria to the new material. Thus, a course in sex is different from a course in history only in content. The procedure is the same.

The student learns the material, takes a test, gets a grade in the grade book, and lives happily ever after. Unfortunately, this is not what the lawmakers had in mind when they mandated the course.

The progression of drug education will serve as an example. In the late 1960s several states passed laws requiring a specified number of minutes of drug education for each student per week. School administrators responded with confusion. The first question was who should teach it. In most cases, drug education became a science class, and the study was largely pharmaceutical. The teacher discussed the drug makeup of each pill and pointed out the usual reaction. Students, particularly the drug users, kept detailed and accurate notes. In the more progressive classrooms, policemen came to class and burned marijuana so the students could identify the smell. Most agreed that it was marijuana, all right. Drugs were studied like history, except with more intensity. The teachers lectured; the students studied and took their tests. We were successful—in educating drug users—but we weren't achieving what the legislators had in mind.

Our next attempt was the scare technique, and the course became more of a social science class. We invited the reformed addict in to challenge our students with horror stories and dirty words. We showed films of deformed babies, and we sponsored poster contests. This procedure didn't work either. Students are too sophisticated to learn from cheap propaganda.

The most recent attempt at drug education has been in the form of values. We are trying to put students in touch with their personalities and values, assuming that drug use is a by-product of something deeper and more profound within the person. Thus, we engage in such activities as making paper sack masks of our "inner selves," deciding whether we love our mother more than our father, and making a list of twenty things we like to do in our spare time. If we are really current, we don't mention drugs, and we don't criticize any feelings or actions. We are simply trying to put the student in touch with himself and his personal valuing equipment.

It is not my purpose to criticize any of these procedures. For a given student and with the right teacher, any procedure could be good education. But I want to illustrate the fact that schools have been given tasks they are not prepared to meet.

Teaching a child to read is a qualitatively different activity from applying social salve. We don't know as much about how to teach reading as we need to know. We are definitely not prepared to bind the wounds of a changing society.

There is a very subtle trap here; and unfortunately, some very fine educators, even some Christian educators, have been snared. There has been creative thought invested in designing efficient and ethical techniques for schools to teach values, but that is not the issue. The issue is the educational costs of such programs, regardless of how effective they might be. The issue is still concentrated on reading scores, composition skills, and standardized test scores. It is naive to assume that the schools are equipped to cure social ills when they haven't even mastered their original purpose—cognitive and intellectual development.

All this responsibility for social doctoring presents a rather interesting paradox. It comes at a time when pollsters tell us that the public has lost confidence in the schools to fulfill their roles. Yet lawmakers and the public alike are still thrusting them into added and more difficult tasks. The schools are in a no-win situation, and most school people are aware of this. They need help. There is still a big gap between football offenses and haircuts.

The Deteriorating Family

The nuclear family may not be a dead institution, but it is definitely not the picture of health. The statistics are provocative. Nearly one-half of all marriage contracts are now broken before they reach maturity. More than 40 percent of all children enrolled in school come from a home of fewer than two parents. These are national averages. In some neighborhoods and communities the percentages are even greater.

But cold statistics are based on living realities. In fact, we have heard those statistics so often that we run the risk of becoming insensitive to their meaning. Behind each statistic is a human being who deserves our sensitivity. The father-child relationship is so sacred that it serves as the metaphor of a person's relationship to his Creator. Yet, I have known children who have had as many as four different fathers before they reached junior high school. How many times can we rip such a sacred commitment from a child's life and expect him to keep his stability?

One spring day, I was standing in the hall of a junior high school when a student came merrily along, whistling a happy tune. A teacher stopped him and said, "We missed you in class yesterday."

The young man thought for a moment, and then reported his absence. "Oh, yeah. I forgot to tell you. My real dad died out in Iowa, and we had to go to the funeral." With that he continued down the hall, whistling his tune.

I am simply not prepared to teach in a world where young adolescents are so emotionally confused that they cannot grieve the death of their own fathers. (That incident was particularly painful because I had a son the same age.)

Even families which escape the statistics have their problems. A newspaper columnist's survey revealed that 70 percent of the parents who responded would not have children if they had the choice again.

While the next section of this book will deal with some of the problems facing the family and some possibilities of correction, the point here is simply that the family is not a dependable educational agent.

This is more disturbing than it sounds. For two centuries, the American schools have worked hand in hand with the family in rearing children. They were, for the most part, mutually supportive agencies. Children knew about this relationship, and they knew they could depend on it. Several of us had this confirmed when our fathers said something like, "If you get spanked at school, you can expect the same when you get home." We probably suspected a conspiracy, but we realized the unity of authority, the total cooperation between home and school. Now in many homes, if there *is* a home to care, that parental statement has been modified to, "If you get spanked in school, we will call the lawyer when you get home."

For two centuries the schools have depended on the family to teach children some important lessons about life—response to authority, the desire to learn, the value of honesty, the meaning of respect, the purpose of punctuality—and now there is no family, at least not a dependable one, to teach those lessons.

School people are baffled. For one thing, our excuse is gone. I personally have invested many hours in teachers' lounges camouflaging my inabilities as a teacher with such statements as, "I don't see how they expect me to teach in this school. I am not getting any help from the home." The declining home is so obvious that the excuse has lost its power. We are either going to have to work around the missing family or find a better excuse.

The common response to this immense problem is rhetoric—hours and hours of it. It is now popular for writers and speakers to get on their soapboxes and decry the deteriorating family, just as I have done. It is also popular to enumerate all the social damage caused by the deteriorating family and to imply that the only barricade to the tragic route we are on is to have a magical rebirth of the "good old days of hearth and home." It does make good rhetoric—the teary-eyed kind, filled with a strange mixture of nostalgia and hope. But that is probably not going to happen, not for a long time, at least not in our lifetimes. The institution of the family has been deteriorating for years, and it is not going to be reborn instantaneously.

Schools are actually caught in the middle. Without the family teaching its designated lessons, educational systems aren't as effective as they should be. The normal reaction would be for the schools to try to correct the problem or at least try to compensate. So they have attempted this in two ways. Schools, in many instances, have tried to become a substitute family—to fill the gaps created when the family doesn't exist or isn't functioning as an educational agent. Many administrators aim their extracurricular programs at these gaps. They reason, "If the child can't go home, at least he can go to the gym for basketball practice."

The other way in which schools have attempted to correct the problem of the missing family is to teach young people the importance of family relationships and values.

Schools often offer complete courses in such things as home, values, family relations, and family living; and some of these courses appear to be innovative and exciting, at least on paper. But they all suffer one possible pedagogical weakness: In order for young people to learn these lessons, they must have role models, they must come from homes—or at least *know* about homes—where the textbook values are being applied. Many young people don't have access to such models; so in these cases, schools seem to be teaching impractical ideals.

Both these attempts by the schools—to become a substitute family and to teach family values—have met an avalanche of criticism, some from guerrilla fighters and some from organized movements. The opponents protest that schools aren't designed to teach these kinds of lessons, that the original purpose of schools is being weakened, that the homes should teach the values and the merits of successful family living.

Most educators agree, but they have been forced into their

roles. This is the paradox. Society has placed demands on schools that the schools can't meet; yet, when the educators do attempt to meet those demands they are criticized for their efforts.

A search for a solution to this dilemma brings us back to the underlying thesis of this book. Your child is going to have a better chance of surviving and perhaps even thriving in the world of adolescence if he can get a sense that the school and the home are working together toward a common end.

By this time, I hope that you are becoming familiar with that mysterious monster called the school. I hope that you are familiar enough with the school and with the general attitudes of teachers that you are at least not afraid of them anymore. I hope you are familiar enough to begin to believe that most school people really do have good intentions despite how it may seem to an outsider. I hope that you are familiar enough with schools to be an agent of positive correction should there be something which needs correcting.

Now that you know something about the schools, it is time for you to begin to understand another major force in your child's education: his parents.

PART II

THE POWER OF THE FAMILY

In every small town I have ever known there is something I call the "town family." Although each town family is distinctive, there are some general traits. First, there are too many children; usually, this is the largest family in town. Their house is the most unbecoming in the community—old, in need of repairs and paint, and ill-kept. Generally, the family has some really despicable habit which contributes to the blight. They keep chickens or rabbits or have a huge population of dogs and cats to match the children. And there is never any grass in the lawn. It is worn bare by traffic. Old, abandoned cars become the only decorative items.

The children live with independence and mobility. They have no first names when they get away from the house. The community knows each as "one of those _____ kids." Teachers sometimes don't even call them by first names. The children pick up odd jobs, hunt for pop bottles along the road, and accept handouts.

Father's salary is never adequate, so the community begrudges them luxuries. If the family gets a new possession, such as a TV, the community gossips, "What do they need with a TV? Why don't they spend that money on food and clothes for all those kids?" Yet, the parents take vacations and weekends away, leaving the children at home to fend for themselves and contributing further material for the gossip mills.

However, when we successful people meet back in that town

for ten-year reunions, we are always surprised. One of those children is now a doctor, another is a lawyer, another is a space scientist; the girls are all happily married to upstanding people. At the frequent family get-togethers, the whole block is covered with big cars and happy people. Sometimes we can gossip about this all evening.

Since I have seen this happen so often—children rising out of obscurity and deprivation to meet life and conquer it—I have tried to look for a pattern, a hint. What was it that indicated that these young people were going to grow into healthy, intelligent, success-oriented adults? In retrospect, I think I have discovered something. In every case, these children demonstrated a deep and abiding loyalty to family.

While the rest of the community was telling me what a desperate scoundrel the father was, the children were quoting him in class as if he were the ultimate authority on matters. Mother worked, but she also darned the socks, washed the necks, and refereed when she thought someone was taking advantage of one of her children. In school corridors, older brothers and sisters would stop and tease the younger ones, even when they were avoided by most of the other children.

At one time in my life, I thought those parents had so many children because they were ignorant. Now I've decided they had so many children because they had a great capacity to love.

As a parent, I have worried about what gifts I can give my children—an education? decency? an appreciation of the value of hard work? straight teeth? a knowledge of God? a color television? an automobile at sixteen? But in the light of what I have learned from all the town families I have ever known, I wonder whether I can give them a feeling for the spirit of family. I want to, and it is from this desire that I write this section.

This is a presumptuous undertaking. I still have children of my own who have not yet glorified their parents in adulthood. But I have some opinions which I have formed through working with other people's children. Let me share the best of those and hope with you that we can all fulfill the mandates of our office of parenthood.

5

"I Wish I Had Never Been Born Into This Family!"

For the Christian, the first line of defense, and possibly the ultimate line of defense, against the problems and inadequacies of the public school is the family. This statement is not really a contradiction to the preceding chapter about the declining family. It is true that the nuclear family is a very feeble institution in contemporary society, and it is probably also true that it is not about to encounter some miraculous and instantaneous recovery. But for the parent who is concerned about the quality of life for his children and the quality of their preparation for adulthood, strengthening the family remains the number one priority. Throughout this book I make suggestions about how a Christian can have some input into what is happening in the schools; but all this input still doesn't guarantee that the child is going to be well-educated. Despite the specialized nature of human services, the parents are still the primary educators—not the teachers and not the schools.

The logical reaction to a discussion of family is, "Do we really need this discussion? After all, people have lived in families for hundreds of years without any specific instructions or any how-to books. The nuclear family has survived wars, pestilence, disease, and time. Why do we need special help in practicing the craft now?" Unfortunately, the statistics indicate that we *do* need help.

Conditions have changed. In the past, the family has been a natural social institution. But it isn't anymore.

Finding the Nucleus

By definition, the *nuclear family* has a nucleus—a center, a heart, a hub, a vibrant and dynamic organ around which the family moves and finds its identity. A philosopher suggested that community results when the members relate to a *common other*. If the family is a community (or a unit of people who communicate), it must have a definite common other to which all members relate. I am willing to take this idea further and maintain that all members of the community must be equal distance from the common other. In other words, if I place some common other first in my life but my wife places it third and my children place it fifth or even lower, we won't have much of a community or family life. We must relate to the common point from equal distances; and, preferably, it should be the number one priority for each of us.

What, then, is the nucleus of your family? What is the heart or the center around which all members move? Is it a house? Probably not if you are an average family. The house is viewed as an investment or a stepping-stone into a nicer house.

Is it the father's job? Perhaps so in your house. But I have talked with children whose fathers are high-ranking executives in some of the most powerful firms in the nation. When I ask them what their fathers do, they report, "He works in the Loop." Translated, that means he gets on a commuter train every morning and disappears into existential nothingness until seven o'clock that evening. These men may be controlling the destiny of the nation, but their own children have no concept of the nature of their work or its importance.

Historically, throughout the Western world, the nucleus of the family has not been so elusive as it has become in recent years. I was reared on a farm (and in an earlier generation). Every member of the family knew what was the center of life, and we all related to it equally. We knew what ultimately made all decisions. Those decisions might have been interpreted by our mother or father, but the *farm* made the decision. The farm decided what time we would get up, when we would go on vacation, whether we could buy something, whether we could participate in extracurricular activities. Since the farm had almost complete power over our lives, we gave it a large amount of our devotion. It was first in our minds as well as first in our lives.

I saw this same theme in the movie, *The Hiding Place.* The ten Boom family revolved around the clock shop. Those children *knew* what their father did because they could watch him do it, and they could rejoice in his being good at his work. If your children have that rare privilege, you are fortunate. Most don't, thus, we have to look deeper to find that vital organ—the nucleus.

The next logical question is whether this nucleus has to be tangible, a thing. I would like to answer with a resounding no, but I am reluctant to be so enthusiastic. It would be nice to think that people can be united around a noble theme such as love, commitment to God, or even ethical integrity. But I am not convinced they can be. I have heard pastors proclaim that the only way to keep a congregation working together is to keep it in debt. That is a rather strong commentary on our confidence in the power of God moving throughout the membership. But most communities and pseudocommunities to which I belong manufacture artificial tangibles to promote harmony and cooperation. Most Sunday school classes feel the need for a social event occasionally.

Some family prophets have proposed this same kind of artificial nucleus building, and some families have used the advice with good results. For example, family counselors suggest that we reserve one night a week for "family night." In certain families this special night has become quite successful. All members work hard to stay free of other commitments for that night, and the family plans as a unit and plays as a unit. This may sound like a token attempt, but if Thursday night is the only thing a family has in common, thank God for Thursday night. At least, these people have some kind of a nucleus.

In my profession, I encounter families in which a central cause is an activity of one of the children. Sports commonly serve this function. If one of the sons is a football player, the family spends its togetherness and finds some harmony in that football career. Family members wait for meals until practice is over, travel together to the games, and generally plan their lives around the schedule. Again, this may sound like a token effort, but if families find unity in this, thank God for football.

I am not trying to be a prophet of doom, but there are two obvious points we all must accept: 1. The nucleus of your family, if your family is a fairly typical suburban or urban household, is not a natural consequence of your coming together and living together. It must be determined and specified. 2. There are more things in your environment to splinter your family than to bring it together.

Some of these splinter agents are obvious, but most are quite discreet. You pledge a measure of loyalty to them quite innocently; but before you realize it, they have split your family into a thousand directions.

Clubs and organizations, despite their worth, have this effect. Who among us has not had the experience of planning a rather exciting family outing before we realize that it's the night for the Girl Scout meeting?

Some churches are excellent splinter agents, particularly those active churches. A family could easily sacrifice one member each night of the week and avoid ever spending any time as a complete unit. One child goes to Awana on Monday. Mother attends the ladies' group meeting on Tuesday. The whole family may go to prayer meeting on Wednesday, but children frequently have their own session. Father works in visitation on Thursday. Another child goes to a youth meeting on Friday. The parents attend an adult picnic on Saturday. On Sunday, they all go to church, of course, but the young people sit in a specified section, rows away from the parents; and they all listen to the preacher deliver an inspiring sermon about the need for a strong family.

I am not denouncing church work or the Girl Scouts. I am only suggesting some possible problems.

Frequently, our own opulence is a splintering agent. In this generation, most American families are using more space than at any other time in history. Recently, I was visiting a young couple with two small children. They were planning an addition to their house because they just do not have enough space. I agreed and was feeling sorry for them until I realized that the parents who built the house had reared six children there. We are living in a different age, but space separates us.

Central heat is a splinter agent. When we lived in that old, breezy farmhouse that was heated with one small, coal stove, the family met on regular occasions. As soon as we got up, every time we came into the house, and right before we went to bed, we had family meetings—right in front of the stove. Our meetings weren't called or planned, but they *were* functional. With central heat, members of the family can disappear and not surface for days.

The space and heat of opulence is deceptive. I suspect our generation, those of us who are now parents of adolescents and children, grew up watching too much "Leave It To Beaver" on television. Somewhere I got the idea that a good family is one that provides a room for each child; and that in good families each child goes to his room to study, to play, to contemplate, or to wait for dinner. For years, I tried to run my family with this mistaken notion. After all these years of fighting children, I have finally in-

terpreted what they are trying to tell me. Good families have a
family shrine, an altar, a central meeting place; and in good families children like to spend most of their time at the shrine. This
shrine may be the television set, the living room, the dining room
table, or perhaps even the parents' bedroom; but it is the central
meeting place, the replacement of the old, coal stove. It represents the family, and the children go there when they need support or just want to feel warm.

This isn't without problems. In fact, it is sometimes hard to understand because you may get a conversation such as this:

"Mother, make sister be quiet so I can study."

"Why don't you go to your room to study, dear?"

"Because I want to study here."

"But it is too noisy here."

"I know it. Make her shut up, will ya?"

Don't try to figure that out logically. Logic is in the mind, and
that conversation grew out of the heart. Be thankful there is a
shrine which is doing its part to fight off the splinter agents lurk-
ing in the woodwork.

Although my mother doesn't have children at home anymore,
she has learned this lesson from her dog. She pours the dog food
into his dish in the kitchen. However, throughout the day and
evening, the dog will run into the kitchen with a sudden urge,
grab a huge mouthful of dog biscuits, rush back to the living
room where my mother spends most of the day sewing and
watching television, spit the excess biscuit on the carpet, and then
proceed to eat his meals at the family shrine. He knows the
meaning of togetherness.

All this can be summarized in a few simple sentences. If your
family is going to work, you have to *make* it work. It won't work
by accident. If your family doesn't work, all the other energies
you spend trying to control and direct your children's education
will be so much wasted effort. Begin today. Identify your nucleus.

If you don't have one, build one. To that end, let me offer a few suggestions. None of these come with any kind of guarantee. They are only things I have observed other families use with success.

1. Develop a Daily Ritual of Family Devotions. I know this is the same sermon the preacher has been yelling for years, but in this age of space and splinters, it is not bad advice, both for the spiritual and family aspects. You don't have to be a master teacher or a theologian. Just meet and read some Scripture. If you can't read, play a tape. The important thing is the meeting, not the message.

Once, I asked a junior high, Sunday school class who was, in their opinion, the best teacher they had ever had. A brother-sister team answered spontaneously and almost simultaneously, "Our father."

Since the father had never taught in our Sunday school, I decided that we were overlooking some good talent. (Any person who has ever participated in a Sunday school program becomes at some point, the world's greatest scout as well as the world's greatest persuader.) But this father refused to budge. He protested that he was shy, inexperienced, not knowledgeable enough, and he trembled at the thought of appearing in public.

I really think he was accurate in his appraisal of himself, but I think the children were accurate in their appraisal as well. Here is a man to be admired, a parent who can communicate with, inspire, and teach those people who know him best. That is quite a testimony. We have educational programs to train ministers to communicate their faith to thousands of strangers through the electronic media, but only God and our own children can teach us how to do family devotions.

2. Eat At Least One Meal a Day Together. Recently, I asked a group of college seniors to identify their most memorable childhood experience. One stable young man who is a member of

a large, working family answered, "Breakfasts." He explained
that the family met at breakfast each morning to discuss the day,
catch up on the news, share, and eat. To him, it was more than
breakfast; it was the family. I know this isn't always easy to do,
but making a family work is never easy. You have to start somewhere and pray for God's blessing.

3. Develop a Family Hobby.   Be careful not to force this, but if
the parents and children can find something they all like to do,
this can become a great nucleus. I know one family where each
member jogs. As crazy and clannish as joggers are by nature, this
makes the ideal hobby. They come together in their reading materials, their pains, their joys, and their races. In addition, they
are all in good health. Other hobbies that can accomplish family unity are such things as rock collecting, model building,
doing needlepoint, and painting. The beginning of the hobby can
come from two directions. It can be parent-initiated or child-
initiated. If you don't have a family hobby, you might begin by
studying some of your child's interests. You may find something
broad enough to get the whole family involved.

4. Get a Family Pet.   Animals frequently provide good therapy,
and they can unite just because of the demands of care.
    Pets are good instruments for teaching such family lessons as
unselfishness. When the necessity of the dog's trip outside coin-
cides with a favorite television program, someone has to experience the sacrifice of love. Some psychologists are recommending
pet therapy for emotionally disturbed children.
    One parent whose children satisfactorily endured maturation
during the difficult late sixties told me that he attributed all the
success to the family horse which demanded much attention that
would have otherwise been misdirected.

Besides, pets serve as excellent workbooks for the lessons in sex education which most parents dread.

5. *Take a Family Vacation.* Again, be careful about forcing children to go somewhere they may not enjoy; but a well-planned vacation might be the highlight of your child's youth. If you can't afford such a vacation, borrow the money. Financial problems will always be with us, but our children soon grow up and leave. Camping families rank high among the happiest families I know.

6. *Share Your Work with Your Children.* This may not be in line with the pastor's advice, but I have never been accused of being predictable. I have heard those protests that we should leave our work at the office if we want to insure mental and social health. But if a parent is happy with his work, he will want to share it. He will want his children to know the pleasure of being productive, and he can invite the children to help with some of the tasks. They can feel that they are part of the economic scene as well. If the parent is not happy in his work, that is another kind of problem.

In our family, my profession is the nucleus. Regardless of how chauvinistic that may sound, it is a reality. My wife and children know where and what I teach. They know my students. They know my strengths and weaknesses. They help open our home to students; they help me prepare materials. They visit my office and classroom. They plan their activities around my teaching schedule. Thus, they have no quarrels about spending my money or basking in whatever glory might come as a result of my career. We are a family.

Finding Your Nucleus: A Family Test

If after the previous list, you are still having trouble finding the nucleus of your family, let me offer one further suggestion, a family exam.

Call your brood together and get them into a less-than-hostile mood. You may want to feed them ice cream and cake or tell them you have just bought a new car or whatever it takes to make the group cheerful. When you get the proper atmosphere, suggest a family game. You may distribute paper and pencil and let them write their answers, or you may want to rely on the old family-circle discussion device. The method depends on the members' ability to share their feelings with each other.

Now suggest the following activities. You may not want to use all the examples, but the first rule of teaching is to be overprepared, so at least have the whole list available.

1. *Tell us what you would miss most if you were held hostage for 444 days and could not come back to this house.* (Make sure you point out that the family member is only held hostage from the home. Don't deny him his right to Americana such as hot dogs and discount stores.) Now study the answers you get to this question. You may be able to see a trend. Are they going to miss family members and relationships, or are they going to miss things or events? I am not going to make any generalizations about what those answers mean. I would have to know more about your family before I could do that. But you can tell from the direction just what stands out.

2. *Recall some past year and something significant about it.* How far back you go depends on how old your children are. Don't go back beyond anyone's memory. Again, consider the answers. See what is remembered, check to see what will be left when the present passes into the past. What a person remembers tells us a lot about what is important to him. Incidentally, now that my siblings and I have all become senile and grumpy, we play this game by the hours. It is fun to see how our perceptions of a given event compare.

3. *Remember some moment or event when someone in the family embarrassed you.* The answers to this question will tell you what the member values personally.

4. *Remember some moment or event when some family member made you happy to be part of this family.* This will give you the same kind of information as number 3.

5. *Make a list of do's and don't's of child rearing.* Make sure your children participate. Tell them to think about what they are going to do when they have their own families. I suggest this only if you have the courage to hear the truth. Remember that children can be quite candid.

In "The Death of the Hired Man," Robert Frost wrote, "Home is the place where, when you have to go there, they have to take you in." That family exam should help you identify what there is about your home which makes the family members come home when they can't go anywhere else, and this is the nucleus. I was weened from the house of my youth more than twenty-five years ago. Yet, about twice a year I load the whole family into the station wagon and drive more than 2,000 miles to see my mother. But I must confess, I am not sure which I miss most—my mother or the farm which was and still is the nucleus of our family, the backdrop for all our memories.

In the next two chapters I am going to contend that the family is the major educational force in the lives of most well-adjusted, happy young people. I am going to suggest that despite the pervasiveness of television and compulsory schooling your child's parents are still his most significant and memorable teachers. But if you are to meet that challenge, you need to know how and why your family works. You need to know where to find the center.

mented such a program, there is a room designated for students on suspension. The students come each morning and report to the room where they spend the day, suspended from class and other school activities. Teachers are assigned to supervise that room. I suspect that principals in charge of in-school suspension search their faculties for the most ill-mannered folk, but teachers tell me that they are assigned to supervision duty as a part of cruel and unusual punishment for teachers. Nevertheless, the students are forced to sit in the room without the privilege of socializing with their colleagues and without the privilege of participating in classroom activities. When they have served their specified number of days, they return to their normal routine.

According to administrators who have implemented such programs, the in-school suspension is an effective technique for controlling student behavior. But that is not why I brought it up. Rather, I am interested in why school people saw a need to shift the location of the suspension from the home back to the school.

When officials suspended students from school and sent them back to their parents, they thought they were doing more than just protecting themselves by getting the disturbance out of their hair. They thought they were doing more than punishing the student. They really believed that the parents were going to teach these students something important about cooperative living.

Evidently school officials don't believe that anymore. If they just wanted to be rid of the problem, it would be much easier to ask the student to leave for a few days. Supervising in-school suspension ranks right up there with collecting lunch money and zippering galoshes among teachers' favorite things to do. A principal doesn't win many friends by telling faculty members that they have to sit in that room with all the discipline problems.

But it is apparent that school people still want those students to learn something about socially acceptable behavior while they are being punished. And it is also apparent that the educators feel those lessons are now better taught in school rather than at home.

This reasoning bothers me. It may be true, but it still bothers me. For centuries, school people have depended on the home to teach the students certain integral lessons. And if those lessons were taught at home, then the school could more effectively teach what it was designed to teach. In spite of all we may know about social relationships and learning theory and educational methodology and human values and behavior modification, not all that much has changed. Basically the schools are doing what they are capable of doing; but there are some lessons, some very important lessons, which they cannot teach well. If your child is going to learn these lessons, he will have to learn them from you. And if he learns these lessons from you, he will be in a better position to learn the lessons the schools can and do teach.

If you want your child to thrive and survive in school pause and reflect on what it is you must teach your child *before* he gets to school. Think about what kinds of lessons you would have taught your child if he had been suspended (back in the days when schools did suspend), and maybe he will only talk about in-school suspension secondhand.

To stimulate your thinking, I offer the following suggestions.

Self-Worth

Any teacher who is worth his salt or his salary will admit that he can't teach a child much unless that child has a good image of himself. Some children come to school with a positive self-image—confident that they can master history, literature, or science; but many don't have such an image. Good teachers then make an attempt to build it, but what teachers build is usually self-esteem rather than self-worth. There is a distinct difference between the two. Self-worth results when a person is satisfied with his own existence and does not need to make apologies for being. Self-esteem comes from comparing oneself with someone else and coming out on top.

For the gifted, it is easy. The student who has medals and patches hanging from his athletic jacket has little trouble with a self-image. A shy or less aggressive child has more difficulty.

Teachers attack low self-images with competitive situations designed to let the child succeed. Thus, the result is self-esteem. "Sarah won the spelling bee today." "Joe is the best baseball player in the class." "Johnny is the best chalkboard eraser I have ever had." This is actually good teaching. It is quick, and it gets good results. Students who feel good about themselves, either from self-worth or self-esteem, perform better. They are happier, more pleasant, more industrious. But even the best teacher cannot possibly reach every student with an image-building situation. If your child is going to learn the lesson of self-worth, you are going to have to teach it to him.

This isn't easy. Again, our opulence is an enemy. The best teacher of self-worth is human productivity, justifying one's existence by contributing something to the world. In previous generations, this was an easier thing to provide for children. As a member of a farm family, I became a part of the economic force about as soon as I became aware of my own existence. Because I was alive, we could milk more cows, plant more cotton, raise more potatoes. I knew I was a worthwhile human being because I was producing. On the other hand, your children have been financial liabilities all their lives, and you have to work at not communicating that to them. They suspect it, and any little hint makes them feel guilty, destroys their feelings of self-worth.

This has become increasingly apparent as we continue to postpone adulthood. Physiologically, a person is an adult at thirteen or fourteen years old. This is a biological certainty. Mary was probably that age when she gave birth to our Savior. But culture has changed that. Presently, culture is postponing adulthood as long as possible—hoping to keep people from uniting in marriage, reproducing, or joining the labor force. For some, "adolescence" goes on into the mid-twenties. How long can we stretch the gap between biological maturity and cultural maturity and maintain a sane society of young adults?

I have ridiculed some adolescent's behavior with the put-down, "He's only trying to act grown up," but he *is* probably entitled to a little experimentation.

How are you relating to your children so that they know they are not economic liabilities or cultural castoffs eternally trapped in a holding pattern? What are you doing to promote their sense of self-worth? I have a few suggestions. There are perhaps others, which you can derive yourself.

1. Acknowledge Your Child's Existence Occasionally. Just take time to stop and say, "You sure bring me a lot of joy. I am really happy you are my child."

This is probably most profitable when it comes at an unexpected time. It isn't hard to do if your child has, for some reason, just kissed you on the cheek or has just shown you a straight-A report card. Try it after he has just dropped and broken your hard-earned bowling trophy or spilled ink on the new carpet.

2. Give the Child Responsibility. Children are interesting creatures. They may protest their chores in loud tones, but they find distinction in them. Don't be afraid to trust your children with serious and adultlike responsibilities, and you may not need much more. I heard one person proclaim that bottled milk is the curse of contemporary child rearing. If every family had to keep its own cow, children would be happier and better students. If you don't have a cow, create the equivalent of one.

3. Use Praise Judiciously. If your child deserves good words for something he has done, give them to him promptly and sincerely. But don't brag about him or praise him for insignificant or shoddy production. He knows the difference, and he will see through your game quickly enough.

Sometimes unmerited praise can have serious consequences. The child will actually demonstrate unacceptable behavior in an attempt to balance the situation. For weeks, I worried about a football player whom I was not reaching. I tried several forms of communication before I realized that he was a perfectionist and did not want praise for his performance until it met his expectation. Finally, I began to limit my praise and evaluate as honestly as possible. He began to perform at a higher level, and eventually, he could accept my praise because he was pleased with what he was doing.

4. Learn To Like Your Child. I didn't say *love* him. I said *like* him. Develop an avenue which permits a friendly rapport. This is different from trying to be his buddy or trying to be sixteen again. That is a big mistake. But develop lines of communication with your child so the two of you don't feel awkward about being in each other's presence. You may have to work at this, but it can be accomplished. After all, you are the adult of the pair.

When I was in high school, I befriended a fellow student who had developed a pattern of running away from home. Since he came to our house each time, I found myself involved in the family dispute. Finally, counselors suggested a more wholesome relationship between the father and son. To that end, the counselors further suggested that the two spend time together, doing the kinds of things both liked to do. Consequently, one fall I spent every Saturday accompanying the pair on hunting trips. It was the most discouraging period of my life. The two were together—the way Custer and the Indians were together at Little Big Horn. The father would yell instructions at the son. The son would refuse to obey. The father would then question the son's mental ability. The son would question the father's right to authority.

The father would yell back, the son would pout, and the bird population remained unharmed. By the end of the day, all of us were in tears.

Actually, the counselors had not given bad advice. They had just given incomplete advice. These two needed to learn to like each other. Without this as a purpose, those hunting trips only contributed to the gaps and the scars.

You have learned to like people before. Your child is a person. Use the same techniques with him.

5. *Don't Feel that You Have To Provide a Conscience for Your Child.* He probably has one. If he already feels guilty about something he has done, there is no need for your further comment.

I am always surprised by parents who act shocked when their children spill something during a meal. This is one of the occupational hazards of parenthood. You may as well anticipate it. If you bring your six-year-old to my house for Thanksgiving dinner, he will probably spill a bowl of food. This act in no way reflects on his ancestry or intelligence. I have never seen a child spill food intentionally; I have never seen a child spill food without feeling guilty about it. I have never seen a child spill food without being embarrassed. If your child spills food at my table, you should not feel obligated to correct his moral depravation at that moment.

In fact, many children do acts willfully for which they suffer immediate guilt. I would like to tell you that this is due to immaturity, a part of growing up, that a child has to experiment to find his own boundaries. But I suspect that most of us know the feeling of uttering something for which we are immediately sorry. How I wish I had that comment back and how I appreciate the people who pretend to ignore it! During those moments, my own guilt is sufficient.

If your son strikes out with the bases loaded, he probably

knows what he has done. The image is vivid in his mind. He doesn't need for you to help him relive his moment of fame.

Sense of Belonging

As I followed the unfolding of the tragic story of Jim Jones and the People's Temple, I became impressed with the innate human need to belong and with the measures some people will take to fulfill that need. I also became impressed with the possibility that there are millions who are searching for something to belong to. Everyone needs someplace to go when he can't go anywhere else. The family is the most obvious answer to that need, but apparently it isn't working that way.

The schools have tried to compensate with various kinds of programs designed to stimulate loyalties. A good school is one that thrives on something called school spirit. A good school is one in which the students can feel they belong. This kind of community spirit doesn't happen by accident. It is usually planned and engineered by an astute staff; and for some students, it fills a big vacuum.

But there are some dangers in having schools fulfill this need. A student can't stay in school all his life. It saddens me to see a student who has developed such loyalty to his high school that he can't find identity after he graduates. Frequently, this happens to people with promise and ability. Some find some satisfaction by taking a position as a custodian or member of the staff; but many just loiter, searching for the glory, the sense of belonging, the success and acceptance that was high school to them.

Another problem is that the schools can't reach everyone. Thus, wise parents do not depend on the schools to give their children a sense of belonging. This is, in fact, one of the valuable roles of your family life—to provide each member, regardless of how old he is, with a sense of belonging. Again, it may not be a natural occurrence. You may have to work at it. Because of this I offer the following five suggestions.

1. Be Consistent.   It is easy to be the parent of your child and to express your happiness with him when he has just made the honor roll, or has just run eighty yards for the game-winning touchdown, or has just been made an Eagle Scout, or has just sung a beautiful solo in church. It is easy to be a parent when the child is happy and successful. But who is going to be your child's parent when he does something that embarrasses you and even himself? Who is going to be your son's parent when he comes home intoxicated, or who will be your daughter's parent when she is pregnant? Who is going to be your child's parent when he has the most need for a parent? Your child really doesn't need you in the midst of his success; others are accepting him then. He needs you most when there are no other people to accept him. Are you prepared for that?

You may protest. "My son won't come home intoxicated, nor will my daughter get pregnant." That may be true, and I hope it is; but your child *is* going to do something against your wishes. You can depend on that. The issue is the same. There is just a difference in degree. Who is going to love your child (and who is going to express that love) when he is disobedient?

While I was a principal, our basketball team played at a neighboring school. During the game, two of our student spectators practiced their high-jumping skills in a remote corridor of the building. In the process, they damaged several ceiling tiles. The following day, I rounded up the boys, called their fathers from their jobs, and charged the families with the responsibility of restitution. Since the fathers worked at different ends of town, I held a separate conference for each family.

The difference between the two was overwhelming. One father came quickly. He raved to the son about responsibility, upbringing, family embarrassment, and inconsideration. Finally, exhausted and exasperated, he said to his son, "I don't want anything to do with you. This is your doing. You'll have to get out of it the best you can. I'll take you home to your mother." And with that, they left.

The other father was more poised. He explained to the son, in a firm but mild voice, the embarrassment and the hurt. Then he explained that just as the child would suffer in the event of the father's poor judgment, the father would suffer for the son's poor judgment. Together, they traveled to the other town to correct the mistake.

Christian parents have a mandate of love. We can't restrict our love or our acceptance just because our child is not bringing us glory and pleasure. Our love must be consistent through the bad times and the good. Our children must be able to depend on the constancy of that love and acceptance. We must provide them with an understanding climate for confession, repentance, and restoration. Our Lord has done that for us, and we are commanded to do that for our children.

This is a difficult lesson, but no one ever told you that parenthood is easy. I will summarize it in two questions. Do you really love your children or do you love their ability to fulfill your expectations of them? Do you love your children or do you love the part of yourself you see in them? There is a big difference between the two, and it may mean a lifetime to your child.

2. Don't Be Afraid To Correct Your Child.   In response to the above point, don't confuse neglecting correction with accepting. Your child hasn't confused them. Every day I encounter parents who are afraid to approach their children about some misbehavior for fear the child may respond with hate and hostility. That is a blatant mistake. Children can be corrected, should be corrected, *must* be corrected. They may object for a while, but they will recover. The real danger is in ignoring the misbehavior.

As an educator, I have frequently encountered a student who has undergone a sudden, unpleasant change of behavior. He has done some things that have embarrassed him and the people who depend on him. When I call the child in to get to the root of the matter, I discover that he has been guilty of some rebellious act. He feels that his parents know and should correct him. But until he is corrected, he must continue the rebellious pattern. In his mind, he is socially unacceptable until he has paid for his sin. In simple terms, he is in dire need of a parental demonstration of love through correction.

This is especially common in children of Christian parents because the children have a strong sense of right and wrong.

But there is a right way to correct. Always deal with the *act* and not with the person. I realize that this is almost a cliché, so let me give a specific example. One of the most meaningless utterances in rearing children is the question, Why? I suppose its use generates from a strange American misconception that every question has one simple, correct answer. Parents seem to believe that if we yell that question loud and often, the child can give us one terse, correct, comprehensible, brief reason for the most complex of human activities. Have you ever heard the following conversation? Have you ever participated in it?

"Why did you do that?"

"I don't know."

"Yes, you do. Now I want to know, why?"

"Because."

"That's not good enough. Why?"

"I don't know why."

"Don't you know better than that?"

"Yes."

"Then *why* did you do it?"

"I just did."

"I won't settle for that. I must have a reason."

Obviously this discussion isn't going anywhere. The child's answer is probably correct. He doesn't know why he did whatever he did. Most of us do a lot of things we can't explain. Personally, I run in marathon races, but I have no idea why.

The demand for a reason is an attack on the child. There may be some value in making the child aware of his responsibility and the power of choice in behavior, but this is not the right way to approach it.

Be specific. Tell the child what he has done. Explain to him that it was wrong, bad judgment, a mistake. Point out to him why he can't do such things again. When he understands, work out a suitable punishment which will remind him not to make the same mistake again. And for good measure, hug him after your talk. But whatever you do, *correct him*. Children with good parents expect it.

This whole business of punishment, and particularly suitable punishment, is a tricky one. Some parents who are otherwise thoughtful and sensitive seem to catch a severe case of "stone minds" when it comes to thinking of a punishment suitable to the crime. The first impulse is to hit. Since the seat has become the depository of moral decision making, it usually seems the likely location. However, the impulse to hit is probably first because it is the most primitive. The ancient Spartans bit the child's thumb. That makes more sense since the thumb is one of the things that distinguishes man from animal. At least, they attacked something human. I hit my dog on the seat.

Parents who control the urge to hit still may not have mastered the secret of proper punishment. Too many resort to one form, and when one form of punishment is used too frequently it loses its effectiveness. Grounding your child is an appropriate punishment when he has violated his right to free movement, but not for every parental frustration you are ever going to have. Not permitting him to have guests over is appropriate when he has not cleaned his room. Making him find and write new vocabulary words is appropriate when he has used bad language.

3. Permit Your Child Emotional Experimentation. After having been married more than two decades, I am beginning to understand my wife; and one of the things I now know is that she cannot have a good day every day. Sometimes I come home in the evening and greet her with a loving and tender gesture. She responds with a brusque, "Hang up your coat." I am willing to accept that from her. She is under a lot of pressure. She has responded with emotional honesty. She doesn't hate me, and home should be the place where she can be honest.

Yet, when one of my children practices the same kind of honesty, I may yell, shout, stomp, bare my teeth, and show my authority. But children have the same needs as my wife. They need a place where they can be honest with their emotional status. They also need to experiment with emotions. One definition of maturity is knowing how to respond emotionally to a given situation. Immature people can't become mature unless they can experiment. Your child may say to you, "I hate you," and it may be a fairly accurate appraisal of his feeling at that point. But don't let it disturb you all that much. It may even be a mistake to try to reason him out of it. Just demonstrate through your consistency that you really don't deserve that particular emotion, and he will soon try another.

4. Don't Hold Grudges But Finish Ugly Situations As Soon As Possible. Never forget that you are the adult in the relationship and you should be more skilled in the art of forgiving than your child is. Start the relationship anew on happy terms as quickly as possible.

5. Be Consistent. I know I said that before, but it bears repeating.

Respect for Authority

In recent years we have learned that society is not controlled by law. Rather it is controlled by *respect* for law. Laws alone will not prevent chaos, confusion, or violence. Someone must respect the laws and the people who enforce the laws.

A local high school district built a new building about ten years ago. In the middle of the front foyer is a beautiful, inlaid bulldog, the school mascot. It is now traditional not to walk on the bulldog. Although there are no signs, no barricades, no ropes, students do not walk on the bulldog. During the exchange period, the hall is filled with hurrying students, but all step around the bulldog.

There is no authority which could preserve that inlaid bulldog except tradition. Students avoid the bulldog not because of rules or threats, but because of tradition.

I once taught in a school with a strong basketball tradition which had firm community support. During the four years I was there, I never once had to remind a student not to go on the basketball floor in street shoes. In other schools, teachers and administrators yell themselves hoarse with the same phrase, "Get off the court with your shoes on." But we never had to yell at that school. Tradition yelled for us.

Schools have laws, and school people assume that children come to school with a healthy respect for authority and a desire to live according to the law. If the children do not have this respect for law and order, school laws and, subsequently, schools are powerless. About the only way the schools have of approaching the lack of respect is through force and coercion; and this, even when it is successful, only teaches fear, not respect.

To make the matter worse, your child's environment is filled with role models that contradict respect for authority. The public servants are corrupt, the police are dishonest, professional athletes argue with the officials, drivers cheat at tollgates—the list is endless. Yet, the future of this country and the role your child will play in that future depend largely on his learning a healthy respect for authority. Teach him.

1. Teach the Child a Biblical World View. The Christian lives under the authority of God, and this authority gives the world unity, clarity, meaning, and value. The good life is the one that is totally submitted to that authority.

Your child is not going to learn this lesson in school. If he is to learn it, you are going to have to teach it. If he doesn't learn it, you must accept the blame. Begin by having the child learn those Bible verses pertaining to the authority of God that is inherent in His majesty and genius. Show your children role models who have found great happiness through being fully committed to God's authority. Make those role models heroes with the appeal of a professional basketball player. The Bible is filled with such stories. The biographies of Moses and Daniel are just two examples.

Being a sports enthusiast, I had always thought I knew about the really exciting men of courage, strength, and stamina until I met some missionary Bible translators. Study some of their lives if you want to teach your child the power that comes from being submitted to an authority.

2. Develop Friendships with People Who Have Authority Over Your Child. Let the child see those authority figures as individuals. Invite teachers to your home. Stop and chat with a policeman when your child is present. Have a friendly conversation with a sports official.

3. Accept Authority Yourself. Be a role model. Every time you criticize a referee you do some damage to your child. Let your child know that *you* know the value of authority and are prepared to live with it.

4. Never Take Your Child's Side in a Situation until You Have Heard Both Sides. Again I am not saying your child lies, but some do. If it pays off for them, they will probably develop a pattern of it. Just make sure you get all the evidence before you tackle the authority. Things may not be exactly as they were presented.

Some teachers, half in jest but completely serious, send a note home to parents suggesting a compromise: They won't believe the children's stories about home if the parents won't believe the stories about school. Think about it. You may want to initiate such an agreement with your child's teacher.

A Desire to Learn

We learn most quickly those lessons that are immediately applicable and valuable to our lives. Most lessons taught in schools have long-range values. Teachers talk about the importance of motivation in student success. Motivation comes from the student's ability to see the value of a lesson. Parents have a role, an important role, in helping their children see the long-range value to what they are presently doing. This point will be covered further in chapter six, but I offer a few specifics here.

1. If You Ridicule Intellectualism, Be Ready To Accept the Consequence of Your Child Becoming Narrow and Provincial. Be careful about saying such things as, "I don't know why she's making you learn that. I don't see where that will ever do you any good." "I never learned grammar in my life and look where I am now." And be particularly careful about evaluating learning with dollar marks in such statements as, "Garbage workers make more money than teachers." That's true, but you are helping your child develop a very important and possibly dangerous attitude when you point it out to him. Being a garbage worker is a noble choice of career, but no such decision should be based on dollars alone.

Just remember that great thinkers discovered the polio vaccine, developed electricity, and wrote Shakespeare's plays. Of course, there is a big difference between the pseudointellectual and the real one, and it may be your duty to point out the difference. But be careful that in your zealous efforts, you don't give all thought a bad name.

2. *Let Your Child See You Study.*

3. *Be Interested in Your Child's Academic Work.* Make his school work an important part of family life. Encourage him to talk about what he is learning and help him draw practical applications from those lessons.

The Dilemma

In this chapter I have tried to convince you that if your child is to survive the process of growing up and reach adulthood with some capacity for happiness and love, he will need to have self-worth, a sense of belonging, respect for authority, and a desire to learn. School officials, if they are honest, will admit that they can't teach those lessons effectively, despite all their noble attempts, so the responsibility is yours. Your child must learn these basic lessons of life at home.

But there is no checklist at the end of this chapter. Educators frequently admit, "The more important the lesson, the more difficult to measure the outcome." That adage applies here. The attitudes discussed in this chapter are among the most valuable lessons you will ever teach your child. It is important for you to know how well you are doing. But since the lessons are so important, immediate measurement is difficult. By using the suggestions in this chapter and by maintaining a constant and caring relationship with your child, you can get a dim idea now. Twenty years from now, you will be able to see the results more clearly.

7

"I'll Show You My Report Card After I Have Finished the Dishes for You."

I used to interview prospective teachers for employment. Frequently, these candidates were just out of college with new diplomas, fresh certificates, and wholesome attitudes. Since this was in an era of teacher surplus, each felt a burning need to convince me that he was the world's greatest teacher, highly skilled, efficient, thorough, and compassionate.

Somewhere in the midst of the conversation, I would always ask, "How good were your college courses in education—teaching theory and methodology?"

Now that is a tricky question. Teachers everywhere love to sit for hours and criticize their college education courses. In fact, the inferiority of such courses was the subject of a popular book a few years ago. Many of these young candidates in my interview couldn't avoid the temptation.

In glowing speeches they told me that the professors were bad, that the material was irrelevant, and that they had not learned anything.

As an educational administrator, I didn't want to hire a person who by his own admission hadn't learned anything in his college courses. I wanted to hire people who went to good schools and learned something about the art of teaching.

I was amazed at how many young teachers fell into my trap and talked themselves right out of a job on that point. But I feel the same kind of amazement now when I go to a party and listen to parents broadcast for hours about how stupid their own children are. Since I am considered an educator, parents love to tell me about their children's experiences in schools. And many of them love to brag about how Suzy can't read, Johnny can't cipher, Billy can't spell, Sally can't write. Parents think they are impressing me with how bad schools are, but I already know what schools are doing. I visit schools every day. Instead, what I am learning from those critical parents is how bad parents are, or more specifically, how bad *they* are as parents.

Let's face reality. Regardless of what the school is supposed to be doing, regardless of how good or bad it may be, your child's ability or inability in such activities as reading, writing, and performing math skills is your concern. You may be able to convince me that his teachers are bad, but it is still your child who will not be able to function efficiently in this world. And this is a reflection on you.

If your child is going to reach adulthood with proficiency in the basic skills of learning and living, *you* will have to help him learn them. In fact, if your child is going to thrive and survive in school, you will on occasions, have to supplement the classroom activities. You will have to assume some of the responsibility of teaching.

The Parent as a Teaching Supplement

Until about the time of the Civil War, all instruction in schools was one-to-one. The student sat in some corner of the classroom, usually with his back to the center, and studied from his text. When he had prepared his lesson (or had memorized the materials), he went to the teacher's desk. There he recited as the teacher listened, prodded, and sometimes applied strong reminders such as a swat with a switch. For thousands of children who lived prior to the mid-nineteenth century, this was school. It was a slow, prodding process built on the principles of memorization and recitation.

Through the works of educators such as Pestalozzi and Herbart, more innovative teaching methods developed. The process became more exciting, more student-centered rather than content-centered, more experiment- and interaction-based, and more group-oriented. However, with all the virtues of these new techniques, the values of memorization and recitation have never been fully eliminated. To become educated, children must learn some things that can only be learned by committing facts to memory and repeating them so often that they become second nature. The contemporary classroom is not designed for efficient use of recitation, repetition, and memorization; nor is the contemporary teacher equipped to provide the adequate time for those activities.

Most teachers simply have too many students and too little time. The average elementary class size is between twenty-five and thirty-five. A typical school day is approximately 330 minutes. A minimum of 30 minutes of each day is devoted to administrative procedures such as calling roll and collecting money. Other important activities such as music and physical education take large blocks of the school day. With this limited time budget, the teacher must rely on group instruction for most of the learning. It is a rare privilege for a teacher to be able to spend a few precious minutes in a one-to-one relationship with a specific student.

Some students are able to master the material with a minimum amount of recitation and repetition. We call them bright. Others are going to need some supplementary help, and this is the role of the parents.

Reading

Reading is one example. Most reading specialists tell us that good readers begin their educational success story while they are still in the crib. Parents are encouraged to use language—good language—in dealing with even the smallest infants. Avoid baby talk and meaningless speech patterns. Give the baby a model.

According to those same specialists, one of the best methods of promoting good reading skills is for the parents to read to the child. If you have started that practice, continue it even after the child starts school. The important point here is not the quality of the reading but the quality of the selections. Pick something your child is interested in and develop a pattern. Build some expectations on a day-to-day basis. Your preschool child may not comprehend all the subtleties of a good piece of children's literature, but he will surprise you. Don't be afraid of such things as Tolkien's *Lord of the Rings* or Lewis's *Chronicles of Narnia.* Make your reading sessions a reward or a special time. Promise your child that when he starts kindergarten, you will begin reading the Narnia Chronicles. Thus, he will have some positive expectation of both school and the activity of reading.

Turnabout is fair play. Listen to your child read. Beginning readers must read aloud. In the event your child's teacher is too busy, make yourself available. The kind of reading you do is a very complex activity; but at its most elementary level, reading is saying. Provide your child an audience to practice his reading at that level. Be careful not to be so critical that you take the joy out of it for the child; but at the same time, provide enough feedback for him to make corrections. This is a delicate art, but it can be learned with practice. Stay with it. Learn from your mistakes, but be *available.*

There is one inviolate rule of reading. Good readers are people who have read a lot. There are no shortcuts. If you want your child to be a good reader, you will probably have to supplement his school lessons. I have heard parents criticize teachers when their children cannot read, but this only labels the parent as a person who would rather seek excuses than assume parental responsibility. The teacher is probably doing her part with the time she has to devote to the task.

Arithmetic

Arithmetic lessons will have to be supplemented, also. Following Sputnik, some teachers introduced new ways to teach arithmetic and eliminate all the drudgery of memorization. The idea had appeal, but it was not totally accurate. Regardless of how many calculators you can afford to buy your child, he is still going to need to know the basic facts tables if he is ever going to function in society. And the only way to learn those tables is to memorize them. Some students memorize the arithmetic facts rather easily. Some need more drill. Don't be ashamed, disgusted, or critical about the school if your child is one of the latter. Drill him yourself.

If I sound like an expert on this, it is because I have had recent experience. We wallowed in the slough of despair over our daughter's arithmetic scores until we realized that we would have to supplement her school lessons. We made games of addition, subtraction, and multiplication facts; and we played those games at every opportunity—in the car traveling to Grandmother's house, during television commercials, in restaurants while waiting for our food. All members of the family, even the older siblings, got involved. In a very short time her scores improved and her confidence went up—we had hurdled the arithmetic barrier.

There was some fallout to this. We discovered that we had enjoyed playing those arithmetic games; and when the need disappeared, we had to substitute a new study. We are now learning Latin in those empty time spaces the family fills together.

Writing

As your child gets older, you will need to help him with his composition, another apparent weakness of the school structure. Writing is a procedure for communicating ideas. Thus, if the writer is going to experience the purpose of writing, someone must read his material. The parent is the first candidate. (Of course, if the child does not want you to read his material, comply with his wishes. Some things are personal.) Again, you need to be aware of the balance between too little and too much criticism. The important thing is to be an audience.

One night I worked at my office writing a manuscript. In the quiet, I had a burst of inspiration. My ideas came fast, my fingers worked obediently, and I finished the project. I literally ran home to share it with my wife. She read it and made some nice comments. But I was disappointed with her lack of enthusiasm until it occurred to me that it was two o'clock in the morning and she had been asleep for three hours. That night, I realized the importance of having someone read my ideas immediately. Sometimes teachers cannot provide the immediate reaction your child's thinking deserves. You must provide it for him. He will learn to write, not through drill, but when he knows he is communicating.

The preceding examples are only that, examples. All through your child's educational career, he is going to need some help from you. Don't despair at the inadequacy of the school. Overcome it.

The Special Student

In His infinite wisdom, God created each of us different. It is not my intention to get into the awesome, complex, and sometimes confused field of special education. That is a study that deserves more than a few paragraphs. Rather, I want to mention those very select people whom God ordained to be more gifted with their hands than with words. They are not just valuable to our society; sometimes I think they are the backbone of it. They make my automobile safe, my house strong, my furnace warm, and my refrigerator cold. I suppose I respect them so much because I have absolutely no ability with my hands.

Yet, the public schools have never quite decided what to do with these very special people. If you are fortunate enough to be the parent of one, you are going to have to be especially sensitive to his or her needs. Education, as I perceive it and have described it throughout this book, is disciplining the mind in the use of symbolic language. Schools are necessary to teach people the language of thought. A person who is gifted with his hands may not always be too successful in school. Through diligence and perseverance, he may master enough to get by; but he will never be a distinguished student.

Schools do provide special programs for these students—shop classes, vocational projects—but there is always a stigma attached. In people's minds these are programs for the low-ability students, the misfits, the potential dropouts. Educators will protest this statement, but they can't deny that that stigma exists in the minds of most students and most teachers. Educators may protest that the stigma is inherent in the culture, and that may be true. But that doesn't erase its existence.

This stigma makes school especially difficult for the Christian student with special abilities. I suspect a self-fulfilling prophecy at work, but whatever the reason there are usually more smokers in these classes, more poorly motivated students, more potential dropouts. The Christian student who finds himself in this company will need a lot of love and support from his parents. He will need constant assurance that he is not a bad person because he doesn't get an A in history or is not planning an illustrious college career with a full academic scholarship. He will need to be re-

minded that his Savior was a carpenter, that Peter was a fisher-
man, and that Paul made tents.

One fall a large, senior transfer student entered my British literature class. I had met this young man previously during a
church activity, so I had some data about him. On the first day, I
gave a rather simple assignment. As the others began to work, he
came to my desk and reported that he could not do the assignment. When my face indicated doubt, he further reminded me,
"Didn't they tell you? I'm dumb."

I ignored the statement and asked him if he could adjust the
points on my automobile, a strange, German machine with obsti-
nate tendencies. He asked a couple of technical questions I
couldn't answer, then he volunteered to go to the parking lot to
see what he could do. I readily granted permission. I had been
having trouble with the thing for weeks.

About thirty minutes later, he came back and reported that the
car was running perfectly, following minor adjustment.

I was then able to point out to him that he was, in fact, not
dumb, but very intelligent. Although I had information, he had a
skill and a gift. He had already contributed to my living a happier
life. I hoped I could return that favor.

I have never had a student who tried as hard or was more con-
genial. This young man is now a very happy, successful, automobile mechanic. He shows every indication of having overcome the
attitude that God had cheated him in creation. Unfortunately, we
do teach this attitude. Society teaches it, and schools teach it. If
your child has a special gift, he will need your support.

Make him feel that mechanics or carpentry (or whatever his
particular skill) is a good field. Give him abundant opportunities
to use his craftsmanship for you. Give him tools instead of books
for presents. Make plans with him for the full development of his
talent. Treat that development as you would a college education
for another child.

A Matter of Relationship

I offer the material in this chapter as examples. I cannot anticipate or discuss all the classroom strengths and weaknesses in your child's academic growth. But if you use these examples as guides, you should be able to detect the early warning signs, and you should be able to create some kind of learning circumstance to help your child. If you are still at a loss, consult a teacher. If you have a good relationship with your child's teacher, ask him. He is probably as disturbed about the problem as you, and he will want to help. If you don't have that good a relationship, ask any teacher you know. Good teachers are interested in the same thing as you—your child's maximum development.

Actually, there is a hidden message in this chapter: You must have a good relationship with your child. I really didn't mean to hide the assumption nor did I intend to trick you. But it is basic to this chapter, this section, and this book. Let's look at the thought progression. If your child is going to succeed in school and in life, you must supplement his classroom instruction. To supplement the classroom instruction, you must detect deficiencies and possible problems. To detect deficiencies and possible problems, you must have a close relationship with your child.

When the teacher wants to know the child's weaknesses, she sits him down and gives him a test. That is a little awkward for you. You must gather such evidence from frequent and meaningful conversations or from watching your child do his homework, play games, or read a book.

If your relationship is close enough for you to analyze your child's development, you have already begun the process of supplementation. In all teaching, the quality of the relationship between teacher and student is more important than the quality of the method of instruction.

Without this relationship between parent and child, the material in this whole section on family loses meaning. When you search for a family nucleus, when you teach your child the important lessons of life, when you supplement classroom instruction, your efforts are at the mercy of your attitude toward your child and his attitude toward you. I hope you two like each other.

The Family at Work: Final Note

Recently, I traveled to Brazil to conduct professional workshops for teachers of missionary children. The presupposition that motivates such trips is that I know something about educating children and that I can share that information in such a way that the classroom teachers will be more effective. In this context, two false feelings can develop. First, it is easy to build an exaggerated image of yourself and your ability, but it is also easy to build an attitude about "poor little missionary children who are deprived of a decent education because they have to get their schooling in such limited conditions."

During the week, I stayed in the home of a missionary family with four children. Prior to my coming, the children had decorated the house with bright, cheery signs that directed me to all the necessary spots such as my room, my closet, the bathroom, the shower button, the guest towels, and so on. Each day I discovered that these children had anticipated every need. Every time I wanted something there was a sign directing me. I surmised that we were either playing an interesting game or these were exceptionally sensitive children or I am too predictable in my old age.

Each child had a pet, and each pet indicated no lack of love and attention. Even the parrot was bilingual. Breakfast was scheduled early enough to allow family Bible reading. Each person around the table took turns. There was little commentary but much emphasis.

Part of the evening ritual included group reading of poetry and short stories and thoughts the family members had written during the day. There was also reminiscing about a family vacation they'd had about two months earlier.

Those children attend a school which probably wouldn't merit the educators' seal of approval. Teachers have to meet the awesome task of teaching multiple-level classes—as many as four different grade levels in the same classroom at the same time. There are few library books and fewer magazines. Some of the textbooks are more than ten years old. The bathroom is a "down-the-path" variety. Frequently, the temperature inside the classrooms exceeds 100 degrees. There is a limited curriculum, no overhead projector, no movie projector, and no videotaping equipment. Teachers frequently have to teach classes that are outside their area of preparation.

After watching these children for nearly a week, I concluded that the only things they had going for them were teachers who cared and a family life that worked. In all of my educational experience, I have never seen children as bright, happy, creative, and loving as those. Your children should be so deprived.

Your child's family plays a key role in his intellectual, spiritual, and emotional growth. When you evaluate his progress, you must evaluate the effectiveness of his family.

PART III

POWER OF PEERS

We had never really had any trouble with Brian. He was always a good boy, and he tried hard to please us. He was handy around the house. Oh, we had to nag him about chores sometimes; but he got them done eventually. He was a little better than average student—B's and C's. We always thought he could do better, but we didn't push him too much.

We did worry because he didn't seem to have many friends. He never had kids over to the house, and he never went home with anyone. It didn't seem to bother him much, so we didn't press the issue. We just decided that it was a normal phase for someone his age. He seemed to like being at home. We played a lot of games as a family. His father taught him chess, and they played almost every night.

A couple of times we tried to get him into some friendship-making activities. We tried Little League baseball, but he was so uncoordinated at that age that he never got to play much. Since he spent most of his time sitting on the bench, we decided it wasn't worth his time or ours; so we quit that. We also tried Boy Scouts, but he just never seemed to get interested.

When he went to high school as a freshman, he came to us and said that he wanted to go out for the hockey team. We agreed. That seemed to be a good sign—a sign that he was moving out of his shell and into some social relationships.

Well, we never realized how irregular hockey practice was. Since the high school team couldn't get the rink at decent hours, they either practiced early in the morning (in the wee hours of the morning) or late at night (*really* late at night). At first we tried to take him. It wasn't easy, taking him to practice and being there to pick him up when it was over. We were pleased when he told us that some of the older boys had cars and could take him back and forth.

For a while, we thought we had the ideal situation. He was finally getting the socialization. We did begin to notice a change in his personality. He was gone from home so much, and frequently stayed out so late. We just concluded that he was practicing hockey all that time. He did become more antisocial at home. He rarely entered into the family games, and he spent a lot of time in his own room. And he became short-tempered. But we just decided that it was because of the irregular hours.

We never realized we had a problem until the police called that night. . . .

* * *

Charles was a stubborn child almost from the day he was born. By the time he was old enough to walk he was throwing regular temper tantrums. School didn't change him much—just spread his rebelliousness over a wider area. During his first three years in school, one of us had to go visit the teacher almost every week.

He was never into anything really bad—just acts of defiance. He wanted to manage his own affairs; and he didn't welcome too many suggestions, whether they came from us, from teachers, or from the other children. He was probably a bully, in the worst meaning of the term, but since I hated that word so much, I never really admitted the fact.

He was not dumb; but because he was so rebellious, he never did very well in school. Every time he had homework, we had to force him to do it, and then he did everything with such a flippant attitude.

Secretly, we shuddered when we heard reports of problems other people were having with their teenagers. We weren't managing our son in elementary school. What were we in for when he got to high school? We were doing the best we could—church and Sunday school, activities, family trips, but we weren't seeing much progress.

When he was in the eighth grade, Charles discovered wrestling. He had tried sports before, but never with much success. He was just too individualistic. He was always in trouble with his coaches. But wrestling was different. The two seemed to have been made for each other. Almost immediately we began to see a difference. For one thing, he was an instant success. He won with regularity. He began to invite his wrestling friends over after practice. He worried about his diet. At the coach's urging, he began to take his classwork more seriously. He made sure that the family could come to his matches, and he was genuinely pleased when we were there. He became cooperative and even a bit affectionate.

He breezed through high school with good grades and a good attitude. He won wrestling awards by the dozens, but he also won other awards for scholarship and citizenship.

Now he is in college on a wrestling scholarship and is still winning matches and friendships. What a change that one activity made in our son's life!

*   *   *

Those two conflicting fictional stories could easily be true. Any person who has counseled parents for any length of time has a warehouse of such examples. The problem lies in the contradicting outcomes. Why did an extracurricular activity save one fellow and do the other one in?

Obviously, there is nothing inherently evil in hockey or inherently good in wrestling. Nor are the people in those two sports good or bad. At this point, an activity is an activity. The answer to the contradiction lies deeper than this.

Since we are accustomed to reasoning from example, we look for some point from these stories. The point is there, all right, but it may not be the one we want. From dozens of real life examples just like my two fictional ones, we can conclude that peer activities and peer relationships are among the strongest factors in determining your child's approach to himself and the art of living. But we can also conclude from the examples that there is no guarantee about the kind of influence these relationships will have.

Some are positive; some are negative; some are even destructive.

Here is the dilemma. Your child's selection of friends and activities could have a tremendous influence on the kind of adult he becomes, on the kind of life he lives and endorses, on the kind of beliefs and ambitions he holds. Yet, it is almost impossible to anticipate what the outcome of a given activity or friendship will be.

For these reasons, this could be the most important section in this book. As I have tried to deal with friendships, extracurricular activities, and the terrible three of drugs, sex, and alcohol, I have struggled with this dilemma myself. I have even proposed some suggestions for you, but I make these suggestions with the reservation that I cannot predict outcomes. What your child brings to or needs from an activity or friendship will affect what he gets from the activity or friendship. For you to know what he brings to any situation, you will have to know your child. Please read this section with that in mind.

I also want to assure you at the outset that your child's school is deeply interested in his friends, his extracurricular activities, and his relationship to drugs, sex, and alcohol. Probably you share a mutual interest here. I encourage you to keep that in mind also.

8

"You Never Let Me Pick My Own Friends!"

A friend is genuine.
A friend plays with me.
A friend is a person who helps me cry.
A friend is a person who believes in me.
A friend is a person who is faithful.
A friend is a person who accepts me for what I am.
A friend is a person who brings out the best in me.
A friend permits me to make mistakes.
A friend is someone who my father thinks wears his hair too long.
A friend is anyone my parents don't like.
A friend is a person who needs me.
A friend listens.
A friend gets over hurts easily.
A friend is something I wish I had.

* * *

Compiled through a twenty-year career, the list is endless; but it has a unifying theme—everyone needs a friend. During the growing process, children need loving parents and caring teachers, but they also need friends—people from within their own peer group who can provide them with joys and heartaches, a mirror, and a sounding board.

Your child's selection of friends will be a significant factor in determining the patterns of his youth. These are among the most important decisions he will make; yet, you are almost powerless to help him. Selecting friends is a personal matter. In fact, the more conspicuous your intervention, the more futile are your efforts.

Trying to understand the selection is frustrating in itself. Adults tend to select friends based on some rational process. They develop relationships with people with whom they have something in common—vocational interests, hobbies, church, the neighborhood. Usually, when one sees two women shopping together, he says, "That's logical. Those two ladies live in the same neighborhood, and both have young children."

But there isn't much adult rationality involved in childhood friendships. One preschool-age boy will walk through the toys of the boy next door to go further down the street to play. Two youngsters will fill all their waking hours together either playing or fighting—extremes at both ends—but they are friends. Two high school students begin to date, and the teachers' lounge buzzes with "What does she see in him?" A junior high school girl is lonely because she cannot break into a popular but closed clique. I give her wise counsel. "There is another girl in the classroom without friends. You two have much in common. Why don't you get together?" But that is not the advice she wants. She wants me to tell her how to get into the clique.

Don't bother asking your child why he chose his friends. That is like asking me why I like cabbage but can't stand carrots. He doesn't know why. He chose this person for a friend because he likes him. Why isn't that reason enough?

The public schools provide your child with a variety of types from which to select friends. This diversity can be a very wholesome thing. It can serve as both an educational agent and a ministry. You do need to be alert to the kind of friendships your child is making, but you also need to be very subtle in pressuring the child either into or away from a given relationship.

Know Your Child's Friendship Needs

Perhaps the first thing you need to do is to conduct a little amateur psychological analysis. Study your child objectively. Understand how he operates within a friendship. You will be in a better position to help him if he should ever need your help.

Is your child a follower or a leader? If he plays both roles depending on the relationship, ascertain what conditions determine which role he plays. This is important.

In most friendships, there is a dominant and a recessive force. Watch your child when he or she is with a friend. Who decides what games are played? Who enforces the rules? Who sets the standards of dress or hairstyle? Is your child more comfortable with quiet, nonaggressive children or does he or she get into relationships where the other person is dominant?

Does your child prefer relationships with people his own age? younger? older?

All these are keys for understanding your child's friendship needs. Study them carefully.

If you are convinced that you have appropriately taught your child the difference between right and wrong (as you want him to conduct himself), you must further acknowledge that his ability to fulfill that teaching is largely dependent on his role in the friendship. It takes a tough kid to change the course of a teenage action after it has begun. It takes a tough kid to back out of the action and go home when he realizes he shouldn't be there. It is virtually impossible to get out of a speeding and dangerous automobile while it is in motion.

If your child is a follower, you will need to teach him how to get out of a situation before it gets out of hand. If your child is a leader, intensify the teaching of appropriate behavior.

Does your child operate best with one very close friend at a time, or is he or she comfortable with a stable full? One-to-one relationships between children are tender. They are sometimes built on possessiveness and partial "blindness." Children who hurl themselves into a singular relationship will inevitably be hurt. They will need a lot of love and family nurturing during their moments of despair. The first impulse is to teach this kind of child how to have several friends so that one won't matter that much. But that is contrary to his psychological makeup. Just be prepared to minister to him.

Binding Agents

I have already pointed out the futility of trying to make a scientific study which would ultimately lead to prediction and control of your child's choice of friends. But there are some general trends which may help you understand certain allegiances.

Classroom Performance.   One of the strongest attractors among all ages of school children appears to be classroom performance. Good students select their friends from other good students. Average students relate to average students. Low achievers gravitate to other low achievers.

This is evident even with a tightly knit activity. Football players usually associate with other football players, but their friendships are not really based only on athletic ability. The two stars may not be close pals just because they are stars. If a young man is a star athlete and a good student then his friends will probably be from the team, but they will be the other good students on the team.

This sometimes baffles teachers. A low achiever will ask the teacher's permission to get help on a particular assignment. The teacher will grant permission, intending for the person to seek help from one of the more competent students; but that doesn't happen. The low achiever will go to another low achiever for help. Learning results from the quality of the relationship and not from the quality of the counsel.

Activities and Clubs. Activities and clubs are natural adhesives because they unite people of common interests and because they force the participants to spend time together. Usually, we like people if we spend enough time with them to get to know them. In fact, this isn't bad strategy for adults. If I am having difficulty liking someone, I make it a point to spend more time with him. Soon the barriers go down and the friendship goes up.

It is probably not good to encourage a student to participate in a school activity if he doesn't like the other people. If your talented musician just doesn't like the other band members, you may need to help him find another outlet for his gift.

But this usually isn't the case. These friendships develop through the before-school car pools, the practice sessions, the bus trips, the common frustrations and joys. This is where the parents can have some influence on friend selection. You may encourage participation in a certain activity by committing yourself to the activity. (You may have to drive in the car pool rotation, and you will definitely have to wait dinner occasionally.) Of course, you have the task of deciding which school activity attracts the kind of people you want for your child's friends. Somewhere, sometime, every parent is just going to have to trust the judgment of the child and claim God's name for divine direction.

There are some Christian organizations that operate in conjunction with the public schools, and in some places (where the temperature is right) actually operate within the schools themselves. Although there are several of these in schools throughout the United States, I will use Campus Life and Young Life as illustrations. These two organizations minister to high school students. They have young, enthusiastic staffs and exciting programs. Some administrators welcome the staff members into the building during school hours. One explained his reason to me. When the Christian club became active in his school, the vandalism costs diminished by several thousand dollars a year. With him it was sheer economics, but still it isn't a bad testimony as to what such an organization can do.

The staff members are trained to chat with students, counsel, open the Word, and lead exciting regular meetings. When they are allowed to come into the building during school hours, they chat informally with students in such places as the dining hall and library. If they are restricted, they attend extracurricular activities, frequent the local hamburger joint, or meet the students through other students.

It might seem that these clubs provide the perfect home base for the students from Christian homes, but there are some reservations. These clubs do have at least an implied evangelistic mission. If they are populated by too many church-wise young people, the prospects—marginal Christians and new converts—may be frightened away.

There is also the danger of a Christian clique. Any school administrator will confirm that cliques are never wholesome. They are almost always detrimental to the school's overall program, and there are always some injuries to innocent victims who have been closed out. A Christian clique is a particular nuisance. It is contradictory to the Christian concept of "brother and sister."

Don't misunderstand my point. I favor friendships among Christian students, but these young people must guard against closing the membership lest they damage a person and the name of the One whom they serve.

The Church. The church provides the appropriate setting for children to develop relationships with other people who approach life through a faith in the freeing authority of God. Because of the Christian's ability to understand this paradox and to find happiness within it, these friendships can be very strong and rewarding. Parents who are concerned about the kinds of friendships their children make should take responsibility to see that their children attend educationally sound and socially conducive Sunday schools. That may even mean teaching Sunday school for a while.

A problem with these church associations arises when the children in church are not from the same school. This can present a real conflict for the young person who is trying to develop some friendship ties. There is the appeal to commit himself to someone from church to get the value of a common faith and life-style. But there is also the appeal to commit himself to someone in school because he spends a greater portion of his time there.

The apparent solution is for the family to attend church in the neighborhood where the children all go to the same school. The strongest, most loyal, most productive, and most valuable friendships I have ever seen have been those where the children attended both the same church and the same school. But this is not always possible. The family will have to supplement in these cases.

The Non-Christian Friendship. There is no particular need for despair just because your child has chosen some friends from non-Christian homes. He has his valid reasons, and these friendships can promote some real opportunities for a two-way ministry. From such a friendship, your child might learn the true meaning of the Christian experience. It is always good to realize that there are nice people outside the church. The distinguishing characteristic of the Christian is salvation through the grace of Jesus Christ—not a set of given behaviors only.

If you have taught your child well, he will keep his standards. This is particularly important when your son or daughter is dating a non-Christian. I know many church leaders who were led to the Lord through a noncompromising girl friend.

The "My Sad Story" Cult. I must conclude this section with a strong warning to Christian parents about the young person who has learned how to manipulate innocent people through the use of "My Sad Story." This person has a sad story—bad home life, a personality flaw such as a learning disability, a rough past with drugs, alcohol, or sex. The story may be true, and the person may really need help. But some people have learned how to use "My Sad Story" to negotiate and control a friendship. Christian youths are particularly susceptible because they are experimenting with the emotions and complexities of charity and service. Innocently and nobly, they are caught up in a situation that brings them unhappiness, tears, and despondency. "My Sad Story" can drain them emotionally, and the Christian commitment becomes a psychological trap rather than the beautiful and liberating experience it should be. "My Sad Story" can manipulate and dominate the life of the one who is trying to help; and if the user feels that the story is losing its power, he might punch it up by slipping into the past with a foray into "sin."

Christian young people are servants, but they aren't psychologists. Parents must help them realize when they are being used. This "friend's" idea of sacrificial therapy may go beyond boundaries of decent behavior.

Some Problem Areas

With your children in the public schools you will encounter some specific problems concerning friendships, particularly with special events. I endorse the role of strong family relations, but there are times when young people need to be with their peers. The postgame celebration party is a time for young people; it is a time when the children want to relax and play together. A family outing is a poor substitute. The postgraduation party is a time for the graduates to be together. On the surface, the purpose of school dances and proms is not to promote dancing, but to provide opportunities for fellowship and social interaction. Children need these times together. They serve a valuable role in the process of maturation, and no parent wants to deprive his child of peer relationships. The child is not denouncing his family just because he wants to be with people his own age during those times.

However, those parties may not be something you want your child to attend. There may be activities that you can't condone—drinking, dancing, public displays of affection. This is the plight of Christian parents with children in public schools. How do you permit your child the opportunity for social development without sacrificing your standards?

The answer lies in substitution, but it isn't an easy answer. If you are concerned about this part of your child's environment, you are going to have to initiate some effort. You are going to have to hold some parties and social events of your own.

I have seen this work effectively. I once taught in a small town where the best postgame party was at the First Baptist Church. Other groups attempted some sock hops and dances; but when the young people, particularly the players, flocked to the church party, the other parties soon disappeared. It took effort, but those church mothers were concerned enough to make it work. Incidentally, that was probably the most solid group of young people with whom I have ever worked.

If you can't get your church interested in having fifty hungry and rowdy teenagers in for a meaningful fellowship, open your home. You might be surprised at the success. Don't be pretentious. Your excuses are not too valid. Don't worry about the appearance of the house. Young guests have a greater ability to perceive and evaluate what they call "warm vibes." They probably won't even notice the worn carpet or peeling paint if they can sense they are welcome there. The rule for the food is quantity instead of fanciness.

Don't get too discouraged if you don't get tons of gushy praise for your efforts. Growing up is awkward enough without the added burden of being sentimental.

Youth is a fulfilling and frightening experience. Your child will need a lot of understanding. Some of it you can provide, some you can't.

Perils of the Playground

There is also a negative note to this chapter. I define prejudice as the seemingly inherent human need for a person to feel superior to another person. The people in Kansas tell Okie jokes; the people in Oklahoma tell jokes about the dumb Arkansan; and the people in Arkansas tell jokes about stupid people from Louisiana. The reasons for these levels of distinction are varied—ethnic, economic, sectional, occupational, and sometimes religious—but regardless of the source of the boundary, they seem to be universal.

Nice people have learned how to manage these feelings. I suppose we could argue about whether they compensate or suppress, but that is irrelevant. Learning to manage such feelings is a process of maturity. Most children and adolescents are not very good at it. I can't explain that either. Perhaps they are just more honest with their impulses. Nevertheless, this prejudice frequently erupts in cruelty, viciousness, and even violence.

Christian children are occasionally the victims. Frequently, these children are in the minority and are obviously different. Any person, regardless of where he resides, is going to stand apart if he attempts to lead a disciplined, scriptural existence, and parents pass these differences on to their children. Sometimes these children are verbally abused, socially excluded, and even physically attacked. This is a universal problem. Although it may not always be the Christian children who are the victims, there are always some children at the bottom of the social heap who are bearing the prejudicial manifestations of all classes above them.

Dealing with this problem requires a lot of parental maturity. The first impulse is to overreact, and this seems perfectly normal. Caring for our children is a basic instinct and assisting them against their attackers is part of that care. But the first rule is: Don't overreact. Once you have mastered this, you are prepared to take one of several courses of action which may or may not be totally successful. Still, success is more likely if you enter the fray with a cool head. One young adult who had been such a victim told me that his parents' poise was the factor that led him through these perils without permanent injury, physically or psychologically.

1. *Realize that the hatreds which lead to the abuse are neither learned from nor condoned by the school or the school personnel.* Don't delay. Tell the teacher what is happening. If she seems uncomfortable, she is probably only embarrassed because she had not discovered the problem herself. If these attacks have led to physical abuse, this can be stopped. Name-calling and exclusion are different matters, but the teacher can use her position to counteract the attitudes that are causing the problem. I know of teachers who have actually used such situations to teach children some very significant lessons about human rights and privileges.

2. *Don't be afraid to confront the parents of other children involved, but do so with a wholesome purpose.* In a Chicago suburb, some young men under the influence of drugs jumped from their car and attacked another student who was walking home from school. He was subsequently hospitalized with some rather serious injuries. That evening the parents, learning the identity of the attackers, went to their homes. There, these Christian people witnessed to entire families about the power of God to redeem lives, and they gave the message credibility by practicing the art of forgiveness. Revenge would have been more typical, but not more effective.

3. *Don't deny your child the right to a full measure of human experience, including some suffering (particularly when you are avail-*

able to help guide him through it). Loneliness is a part of life. En-
during criticism, deserved and undeserved, is a part of life. I am
not proposing laissez faire or sink or swim. I am instead saying
that there is a point up to which some of this activity is a contribution to the maturing process. Just be alert to where that point
is.

Hope in Helplessness

Since the days when Stoics and Epicureans roamed the streets
of ancient Athens, the characteristics and attributes of friendship
have been a mystery, never quite submitting to scientific investigation or logical reasoning. As a parent, you may have a strong
desire to end all that mystery surrounding your child's choice of
associates. But you probably won't. The next chapter on extracurricular activities may offer some suggestions on how to direct
your child's interaction with certain kinds of people, but those
suggestions aren't foolproof. Your child is still enough of an individual to be somewhat unpredictable—or at least let's think he is.

Since this business of selecting friends is such a chancy affair,
your hope lies in the thesis of this section. Make sure you have a
workable relationship (dare I say friendship) with your child—a
relationship that you have built by spending time, quality time,
with him. Then, when the time comes for him to make decisions
about who his friends will be and what those friendships will
mean in determining his present and subsequently his future, you
will be in a position to understand the process and perhaps even
minimize some of the risk.

9

"Hey Mom, Pick Me Up After Track Practice, Will Ya?"

Schools are commonly evaluated on the basis of their extracurricular programs. A good school is one that competes and wins. This fact usually conjures up an image of huge, tough, dumb athletes, supported by tons of money and equipped like the Washington Redskins. But this is a false impression or at least a sad one. Sports are a vital part of any extracurricular program, but good programs and good schools provide a variety of opportunities. A good extracurricular program is one that has a place and a need for every student in school, regardless of his special talents and gifts. It is more than football.

Most schools, particularly high schools, provide extracurricular experiences in music, drama, debate, newspaper and yearbook editing, student government, literary projects, science clubs, and chess clubs as well as sports. The sponsors and coaches urge students to participate. Schools spend a large amount of money on these programs, so they apparently feel the activities have educational value. In the recent, limited-money era, some schools have curtailed their extracurricular activities or have charged the participants a small fee. In every case, the parents and taxpayers have pledged their support to the concept by raising the required revenue. These programs are not only valuable to our schools, they are apparently playing a significant role in our society as well.

Research supports this. Students who take an active role in extracurricular activities usually do better in the classroom. They have better attendance records, are involved in fewer discipline problems, and achieve higher grades. Consequently, schools that provide a broad range of well-organized activities which encompass a large percentage of students usually have some positive statistical data to validate their claims of success.

Also, most educators affirm that success begets success, so they are just as interested in the orchestra performance as they are in the basketball team. A good program is one that is successful year after year in every aspect of its offering. Teachers who have taught in enough schools to gather evidence also affirm that it is easier to teach academic materials in schools with successful extracurricular programs.

The Values

There are several reasons why Christian students and parents should consider active and consistent participation in some school-sponsored, extracurricular program. These programs can provide a benefit both to the student and to the parent and can help each get maximum value from the public school experience.

1. Extracurricular Programs Keep a Student Busy.   I hate to use that old cliché, but idleness is an enemy to wholesome youth. Except in extreme cases, every young person has several hours each week to either waste or invest. Learning wrestling countermoves or banging cymbals in the marching band may not seem like much of an investment; but it beats shoplifting, streetwalking, or knuckle cracking.

Of course, there are liabilities to this as well. The time commitments sometimes infringe on such activities as homework and church participation. The wise parent will help his child make choices and budget his time according to those choices.

2. *Extracurricular Programs Offer the Most Appropriate Setting for Teaching Some Very Worthwhile Lessons.* Some of the lessons which rank high on both the educators' and parents' lists of educational expectations are difficult to teach. These lessons may be simple to verbalize but almost impossible to evaluate in practice. Good extracurricular programs sponsored by thoughtful coaches can provide a setting conducive to learning. Let me illustrate.

A. *A sense of self-worth.* A student can become an important person through his participation in one of the extra programs. Of course, sports have a higher visibility and more hero status, but a student is more likely to find something about himself that he likes in the science fair than he is in the science class. Perhaps I am making a case for the role of competition in building self-image. I have worked in schools too long to be adverse to the idea. I have too many firsthand illustrations of how a young person's life can change when he identifies with some competitive program and achieves some success through it. I have seen drastic turnabouts, an immediate redirection of an entire life-style. Maybe this has been more common in my career because I was in smaller schools where we had greater need of every person. Frequently, I had the opportunity to work with a student who had transferred from a larger school where he had been inconspicuous. We would put him to work, not by design but because we needed him. His entire educational career, and frequently the whole emphasis of his life, would change. Grateful parents often thought we were better teachers, but that wasn't true. We just had a greater need of their child. And since we needed him for football and band, he was also there for English literature and algebra. This does make a case for small schools, but I will refrain from arguing it here. Despite the size of the school, your child can get involved somewhere. That involvement might help him realize that he was created with a purpose.

B. *Value of teamwork.* Frequently, success in an activity de-

mands a certain amount of selflessness. The student must discipline himself to fit into a broader scheme. He may want to go off
on some musical trip of his own, but he knows that will destroy
the quality of the entire arrangement. He must play the notes in
front of him if the orchestra is to sound good. He must learn to
find happiness in the whole rather than in his individuality. He
must cooperate.

Learning to cooperate is not easy. In recent years as I drive on
highways marked at 55 miles per hour, maximum speed, I have
concluded that many people have not learned that lesson. The ra-
tionale for the 55-mile-per-hour limit is that we discipline ourselves for the greater good of this and future generations. But
people can't be controlled with the thought of participating in an
unknown future. The speed limit doesn't work through a sense of
cooperation; it works only through enforcement.

When we realize that we all live on one planet and every man's
trash diminishes us, we see the importance of teaching teamwork.
That's not easy to teach in the classroom. I hope the coach is
working on it.

Early in my career, I had the opportunity of coaching against a
legend. This man had been synonymous with football in that
small town for more than a quarter of a century, and the legend
portrayed him as a man of integrity and honor. When we played
his team, I realized that the truth of the legend was revealed in
every aspect of the game. His players were well-schooled, intense,
competitive, and courteous. Playing his team was one of the privileges of my coaching career.

A few years later, I became acquainted with a young, popular
surgeon who had grown up in that small town and had played for
"Coach." The surgeon told me this story.

Coach had fallen ill and was in the hospital preparing himself
for death. The surgeon went to visit, for what was to be the last
time he would ever see his high school coach. It was a good expe-

rience. They filled nearly an hour reminiscing and remembering. Coach was the kind of teacher who tried to stay in contact with all his former students, so he provided the surgeon with an update on all his friends and heroes.

The visit ended, and the doctor started to leave. Coach called him back and in the quiet of that hospital room made one final observation. "Son," he said, "your hair is too long."

The popular, busy surgeon reported that he did not return to his office, did not even call in. He went straight to the barbershop, because when Coach says your hair is too long, you get it cut.

This is the kind of teamwork that can be gained from good coaching and good extracurricular programs.

Remembering the opening illustration of this book, you may ask why I rebelled at the thought of asking a player to cut his hair. The difference is in the timing. Coach could tell my friend to cut his hair after having taught him for years. That father wanted me to begin my program with that kind of legislation. It is a difference in relationship and marks the difference between good and bad education.

C. *Rewards of hard work.* Talent is a reality. Some people are more naturally gifted in specific areas. Yet, in most extracurricular activities, a student can improve through hard, consistent training. A person with limited ability can make himself functional, and the talented participant can move toward his potential only through dedication.

In contemporary society, it is a rare privilege to encounter the joy of physical exhaustion that comes from having done one's best. Every child should have that privilege at some time.

I frequently attend high school sports banquets. Invariably, when the coach begins to distribute awards and accolades, there is a very special recognition for some nonathletic-looking player who, through hard work, has made himself an important part of the team's success. The coach's comments include such phrases as "dedicated," "intense," "sacrifice," "total release," "above and beyond"; and the presentation is always followed with a large measure of sincere applause.

The lesson is obvious. This young player has experienced the thrill of setting his goals above expectation and achieving them. Probably none of us aim high enough.

D. *Importance of following the rules.* Although all programs work in relationship to rules, rules are most conspicuous in sports. A good coach teaches the athlete to play by the rules for the maximum enjoyment of everyone. If your child's coach teaches something else, reread the rules in chapter three and plan a visit.

3. Extracurricular Activities Provide an Opportunity for Community, Both for the Student and the Parents. Most students join a particular community when they participate in a specific activity. One common, high school game is to make generalizations about participants in various programs. Debaters all wear horn-rimmed glasses and carry briefcases. Wrestlers are always dieting. Musicians have soft muscles and bruises on their lips. Actors are always on stage. Of course, cheerleaders are always on stage too, so it takes a discerning spectator to distinguish between the two. Math club members wear plastic, shirt-pocket liners and carry calculators. Football players hulk; basketball players stoop when they talk to teachers; and baseball players have tobacco stains on their teeth. This game of labeling is harmless enough, but there *are* some general tendencies within each group. That is why it is important for your child to spend some time and thought on his decision to join one of these particular communities. By nature of talent, he will probably have a link to these people, and he will grow closer through association.

The most wholesome approach to a community is interaction. Your child will be altered or directed or influenced by the community, but he will also contribute to it. He will find his identity and individuality by being a part of something.

Because of your child's choice of activities, you will spend time with a given set of parents. If your son plays football, you will probably get acquainted with some football parents. If your son blocks so their son can run, you will have a very natural affinity. With a bit of effort on your part, you can fit right into a community of public school parents; and you can have some positive influence on the direction of the group.

Occasionally, these relationships are formalized through parent organizations. Become a member of these groups. Not only will you be in a better position to support your own child, but you can be an asset to the organization.

4. *Extracurricular Activities Provide an Opportunity for Christian Witness.* Although this depends on the strength of the community and your effectiveness within it, both you and your child can find ample opportunity to witness to the majesty of God's saving grace through participation in a specific program. If you are accepted in the group and are not overbearing in your approach, you will probably find a very receptive throng.

Talk with your child about this. Extracurricular participation is compatible with the Christian faith. He should never sacrifice his religious training or enthusiasm in order to be accepted. This isn't necessary, and the community may need him to speak out against practices that are not in keeping with the Christian lifestyle.

A young Christian athlete went to his coach and complained about the profanity on the football field. The coach admitted his negligence and took immediate action. He called a team meeting, apologized for his use of profanity, and commanded that in the future no one would resort to that language. The team applauded the decision.

I know it is not a case of eternal salvation; but at least, a group of men became aware of one young man's commitment to the Word of God.

In the area of athletics, there are some particularly effective Christian movements. For example, the Fellowship of Christian Athletes is a national organization that has been extremely successful in spreading the gospel throughout public-school sports programs. Its membership includes an impressive list of professional and college athletes who have strong testimonies to share. Each summer, the Fellowship sponsors retreats and camps where young athletes can share both Christ and their athletic talent.

In many schools, there are strong, local Fellowships that provide the athlete with companionship and instruction in the Christian faith. For the Christian athlete, this provides both a ministry and an identity.

There is, of course, the remote possibility that in the clutches of an overzealous coach this could get out of hand. An athlete's religious commitment should be treated as the sacred experience it is and should never be used to win ball games. A coach has no right to appeal to a player's spiritual allegiance for his own success.

5. Extracurricular Activities Provide Some Children with a Necessary Release from Pressure. Some children simply don't know how to play or how to relax. They are intense, serious, and businesslike. For the parent, this may not be the blessing it appears to be. Pressure and stress are enemies of good health, regardless of age. If your child fits into this pattern, teach him to play. Youth is too precious to be wasted on imitation adulthood. There is a lifetime to be serious.

Stress diseases and reactions—ulcers, mononucleosis, suicides—are prominent among the nation's children. Help your child find a diversion. If he is not motivated to do so, make an effort to promote it. These conscientious, dedicated children are real joys, but don't deprive them of their natural youth.

Some Warnings

Even with good things, one can get too much. Extracurricular participation is no exception. There are some warning signs. Some are very obvious. We parents all know them. We are aware of the dangers. But we need someone to remind us occasionally. Let me offer you the list I use to remind myself of how I should respond to my children's participation.

1. Don't Let the Child Get into Too Much. This is a common tendency for a particularly talented child. Some are gifted in everything, and sponsors of various activities put pressure on students. This can only damage your child. It will give him guilt feelings he doesn't deserve. Keep in mind that the state track meet will probably be on the same weekend as the state music festival. (Sometimes I suspect there is a federal law requiring that coincidence.) If your child is good at both activities, there will be a conflict. The only way to avoid that conflict is to make a decision earlier. Anticipate those conflicts before the pressure is put on your sixteen-year-old child. I realize that earlier I called a sixteen-year-old an adult. Nevertheless, he is still some mother's baby.

2. Be Prepared for Total Immersion. Sometimes a student throws himself completely into his extracurricular project. Some programs demand that much time. Musicians have to practice, athletes have to stay in shape, debaters have to research, actors have to memorize—all this takes time. This can be upsetting. His grades may go down; family life may suffer; church participation may be kept at a minimum. At this point, he needs your wisdom in weighing the assets and liabilities. Does the value of the program justify the cost? Remember that idols come in various forms.

3. *Don't Put Unrealistic Pressure on Your Child To Succeed.* Every father wants a star. Every mother wants a fine actress. But your child's happiness is the primary goal. If your child is happy with his bench-sitting contribution, accept it. He probably has a better understanding of the situation than you, anyway.

4. *You Cannot Relive Your Life Through Your Child.* You have already been through childhood and adolescence. You can't reenter it. Don't project your ambitions, your desires, your goals, or your need for thrills onto your child. Being a human comes with pressure enough. No one can be two humans at the same time. Don't overburden the child. Accept what he is and what he does. Don't expect him to perform as you did.

5. *Make Your Child's Participation a Big Deal.* You don't have to overinflate his ego, but give him support. Make his band concert an important event, not because of the quality of his playing but because he is your child. Watch him play his athletic contests, even if he is not the star. Make the *child* important, rather than his accomplishment. That is doubly true if your child happens to be extremely good. Don't let him forget that his achievement is a gift from God, and it is his willingness to use that gift which is to be celebrated, not his success with it.

Good Medicine: No Elixer

Regardless of your child's ability, a baseball bat or a brass trombone may be a cheap investment in his efforts to survive childhood and adolescence and your efforts to help him.

At least, an interest in these things will give him some opportunity for peer association in a controlled environment. That has got to be better than the unstructured peer associations of the street-corner kind.

So when in the spirit of public interest, the television commentator asks, "It's six o'clock. Do you know where your child is?" you can smile and whisper, "Yeah. He's at basketball practice."

But don't shout lest someone hear you. Remember that participation in extracurricular activities is not necessarily a panacea designed to prevent all adolescent behavior. He will probably still act like a teenager on occasions.

10

"Whose Body Is It, Anyway?"

Hesitantly, I introduce this chapter on the terrible three—drugs, sex, and alcohol—with a brief description of the nature of human values and value formation. Your child's relationship to these "sins of the body" is indeed a question of his values, so the discussion is pertinent. But I am hesitant because I don't want to leave the impression that these three areas represent the total of human values. No! In order for us to discuss values adequately, we would need to go a great deal beyond one's response to the temptations of drugs or alcohol. In fact, these things might, in some cases, be treated as symptoms. The value problem could be a much deeper and much more complex one. Frequently in dealing with young people, we need the grace to be able to distinguish between problems and symptoms. Far too often we treat the symptom and wonder why our therapy is ineffective.

To simplify this discussion, it helps to think of a value as a boundary, a limit. In every moral human being there is some behavioral or social boundary that he will not, perhaps cannot, step over. We just can't allow ourselves to be out-of-bounds. Many of us like the risk of moving near the edge, but we can't step across.

I am always fascinated when I discover someone's boundaries. In my career as an educator, I have met hundreds of young people who could never bring themselves to cheat on a test. There was a moral boundary that prevented them from taking a peek or carrying an answer into the test session. But these same young people who were so noble in testing sessions saw absolutely nothing wrong with copying someone's homework, word for word. Now explain that. On the one hand, these people had a moral conviction against cheating. They were actually incapable of cheating on the test, but they could copy homework without feeling guilty. I am not appalled, just fascinated.

For a parent, the underlying questions as you read this chapter are: What are your child's values? What are his uncrossable boundaries?

We establish these boundaries from two basic sources—authority and experimentation. Most of us, particularly when we are young, decide what we can and cannot do because of the authority figures in our lives. Again, as a parent, your first concern with your child's value formation should be those figures. Who are the authority figures in his life—you? teachers? the Bible? coaches? Sunday school teachers? cool peers? popular heroes? the minister? I am not sure I know how one becomes an authority figure for another person. I would like to think that there is inherent authority in some positions such as that of parent or teacher. I would like to think that you have some place of authority in your child's life by the simple fact that you are his parent. I would like to believe that, but I don't. I believe, instead, that every authority figure in anyone's life must first earn the right of authority. In this book, I have related two experiences with coaches and haircuts. In the opening personal illustration, I had not earned the right to be an authority figure in that player's life. I could have exerted force, but forced response has little to do with value formation. On the other hand, the coach in the surgeon's story in chapter nine had earned the right to suggest short hair; and in this case, if the coach valued short hair, then the players valued short hair.

I suppose now that I have convinced you of the above point, I have a responsibility to tell you how to earn the right to become an authority figure in your child's life. That is not an easy task. We are talking about complex standards in the lives of complex people, and oversimplification and generalization could be inaccurate and even dangerous. However, I do think I can isolate some suggestions.

Authority speaks to a person in two ways, by preaching and by example. I am going to avoid the urge to tell you that example is stronger than preaching except to restate the point in the paragraph above. Those who would preach values must live by their words. One of the biggest sources of frustration in the lives of young people is the inconsistency between what adults say and what they practice. As you read this chapter, section by section, ask yourself this question, *Will I be satisfied if my child lives his life by the same principles that direct my life in response to drugs, sex, and alcohol?* I am not interested in what you *tell* him but in what you *show* him.

While you are considering the power of example in value formation, consider another point. Many of the examples to which your child is exposed daily demonstrate a life-style that takes a rather flippant attitude toward traditional morality. Most popular heroes don't endorse virtues such as abstinence and monogamy. TV programs, movies, and biographical accounts of famous people present, at best, a nonjudgmental attitude toward adultery and drunkenness. If your child is going to develop values contradictory to those models, you and your child's school must work together in making that contradictory system appealing enough for the child to establish personal boundaries.

Drugs

Unless you lock him in the attic for about fourteen years, your child is going to be confronted with drugs. It may be incidental and indirect, but there is still going to be a confrontation. Drugs are about as prevalent as oxygen, and parents may as well accept that. I know some people who have almost moved themselves into bankruptcy trying to find a school free of drugs. It is a futile effort. Drugs are in public schools; they are in Christian schools. Let's talk objectively.

Lines of Defense.   Adolescent behavior is dynamic, and it is difficult to describe accurately at any given point. However, drug abuse seems at present to be waning some, particularly in the suburban schools. In the absence of scientific study, I base my position on personal observation and conversations with students. I am told that drug use is more localized, restricted to a specific group of students who tend to identify themselves in rather tight circles. Nevertheless, drugs are still available to any student who wishes them.

   The first question a parent must consider is why a young person would ever experiment with drugs, particularly considering the campaign of negative literature that has been conducted during the past several years. The answer to that may be more shocking than it is intended to be. Many young people first take drugs in a deliberate attempt to hurt their parents. If there is a power struggle, the young person needs the action of drug consumption to gain an upper hand. As one young person told me, "If you can't join them, beat them." The next question for you is *Would my child ever want to hurt me?* It would be naive to believe that all young people who sit around and smoke marijuana on a regular basis are actually motivated only by a strong hatred for their parents, but many experimenters begin there. The edict is simple: If you want to prevent your child from taking drugs, don't give him cause to want to hurt you.

   You may move the family, pay tuition at a private school, or monitor all your child's activities; but your real defense against his drug use is your relationship with him.

   The second major cause of drug use is peer expectation. If your child associates with a crowd who take drugs, he is more likely to become involved. These drug groups seem to achieve a cohesiveness that provides the membership with a sense of belonging. A student who is having difficulty obtaining status within a different group might gravitate toward the drug culture just for the sake of companionship.

This is the first thing parents should tune in to. Know your child's circle of friends and know how he fits in, even if that demands your inviting all of them over to the house for pizza.

Most adolescents have a profound psychological need to belong somewhere, and most will go from group to group until they find that place. When your child complains, "I have no friends," he is asking for help. *Listen to him.*

Drug groups *do* tend to be rather self-perpetuating. Older members win the loyalties of younger students by providing them with a source of drugs. Through this process, the drugs sometimes filter down as low as the elementary schools. Parents should be alert to the dangers of having a younger child build friendships outside his own age-group.

The parents' course of action has already been discussed in earlier chapters, but this reemphasizes the importance of parents' encouraging students to participate in wholesome, peer activities and providing a family climate of love and acceptance.

The parental relationship is not only the major key in prevention, but it is also the first factor in detection. Parents ask me, "How would I know if my child ever took drugs?" The answer is that you should be alert to any changes in moods, attitudes, or behaviors; but that implies a relationship close enough to allow you objective observation. There are some tendencies in those changes—the child is quieter and wants to spend time alone, is defensive and rebellious, or is somewhat paranoid; but those are not consistent enough to be dependable. If you know your child well, you will be able to detect the changes without a road map.

If you think you see changes, you may want to contact teachers and counselors. Remember, school officials don't want your child to use drugs either. Don't be embarrassed. They will respect the concern. In fact, many schools alert parents when they suspect drug usage. Those people won't call you unless they have cause to suspect, so *cooperate.*

There is one word of caution. Remember that your child is still a developing person and that not all changes or impulses or emotional outbreaks are drug-related. Do not panic just because your child decides to sleep in one Friday evening. During the early seventies, some of us became so frightened by the drug epidemic that we couldn't permit an adolescent the right to teenage behavior. Every time we saw a young person having a good time, we just knew he was on drugs. In defense, the young people developed the rather meaningless term "high on life." The more religious ones went a step further and developed the notion of being "high on Jesus." That shocked our evangelical conservatism, but we probably forced the explanation ourselves.

All this caution can be summarized in one imperative—*Don't panic.* Your ability to believe in your child will go a long way toward insuring desirable behavior. Your personal knowledge of drugs is like insurance. You have it, but you really never expect to use it.

Don't make the mistake of overrating the power of prevention in drug-education programs. Through his course work, your child is accumulating a storehouse of facts about drugs; and he probably knows more about them than you do. But facts can't make his value judgments for him. Knowledge alone is no warranty. Don't expect a formal educational approach to substitute for your work as a parent.

Your Civic Position.   Drugs do constitute a social problem, particularly in schools; and as such they become everyone's concern—whether one's child is involved or not. Thus, you must be prepared to cooperate with the authorities.

Drug use is almost impossible to discover. You don't need to make an appointment with the principal to tell him that there is drug use in his school and that he should stop it. He knows that much already. His problem is how to detect it and prove it exists. This isn't easy, and from recent court cases, he has learned one rule: Regardless of what he does, someone will think he is wrong.

If you want your child to attend a school where drugs are either nonexistent or well-hidden, you must cooperate with both school administrators and police when they crack down. This may not always be pleasant. Your child may have to be detained and searched. He may have to open his locker for the dogs to sniff. He may have to watch an unpleasant scene when police arrest someone. If you don't like these procedures, propose some better ones. The authorities are open to suggestions. If you don't have better suggestions, cooperate and support the present efforts.

Cooperate with authorities even when your own child is involved. This is a tough mandate. The basic human urge is to protect your own, even to the point of being dishonest. But that won't get to the problem. Face the issue squarely. Don't try to ignore the facts and don't make excuses. The authorities do not intend to hurt your child. Their mission is the same as yours—to get him through adolescence into sane and productive adulthood. You can demonstrate your parental love by cooperating with them. For example, if your child has bought drugs, he bought them from a criminal. This may be strong language, but selling drugs is a criminal act. The authorities have been trained to deal with the language and the situation.

One Final Note.   If you ever discover for sure that your child is taking drugs, just remember that you haven't come to the end of the world. Don't disown him or decapitate him. If a chasm of love is part of the problem, renewing the love is part of the therapy. During this time, your child needs you more than ever. He may reject you, but he *needs* you. Don't despair. Don't panic. Claim the name of the One within whom you have placed your faith. God is able to keep that which you have committed to Him.

Teenage Sex

Nature and culture join forces in a conspiracy against adolescents. Nature equips them with the desires and functions of human sexuality. Culture restricts their use of those functions.

In many cultures, people assume the responsibilities of adulthood in their teens. They become productive members of society, marry, and reproduce. The American culture discourages this kind of early maturation. We delay the process until the young person graduates from high school or college. This makes sense within our culture; but in the meantime, many adolescents are confused about what to do with their sexual desires.

Many don't survive the conflict. Nationwide polls frequently shock us with exact percentages. A survey taken in 1979 indicated that more than one-half of the nation's teenagers engaged in premarital sex. Regardless of what you think of statistics, the numbers do prove one point: Your child is probably not as naive as you think. If his classmates are figuring into the statistics, he has to be aware of the activity.

This is another tough lesson of parenthood. Sexuality is a difficult topic, and most of us prefer to avoid discussing it with our children. By so doing, we leave them open to seek education from the culture itself.

Through the medium of sex-appeal advertising, through locker-room talk, through pornographic material, culture teaches our children that sex is dirty, mature, mysterious, desirable, on the fringe of decency, clandestine, never innocent, animalistic, sensually rewarding.

There are some organized, educational programs that attempt

to approach the issue of human sexuality at a higher level. Some elementary schools are providing third- and fourth-grade girls information about their bodies through the use of films and sessions with the school nurse. These are very worthwhile films, particularly when a sensitive and trained person such as the nurse or teacher leads the concluding discussion. Frequently, schools will invite the parents in for a screening prior to the actual showing. If the parents do not wish for their daughter to participate, the student may be excused. If your school is using the film but doesn't invite parents to the screening, assume the principal forgot and invite yourself. The cooperation may not be enthusiastic, but it will be sufficient.

There are other formal educational sessions throughout the school career. For example, most high school biology classes (usually offered to freshmen or sophomores) include one unit on the human body. This naturally covers the sexual capacities. As a veteran of nearly twenty years of marriage, I attended one session in a local high school biology class a couple of years ago. I had actually gone just to evaluate a young teacher in the classroom. This day, she covered the male reproductive system. It was the single, most beneficial, educational hour I have ever spent. She covered the material objectively and seriously. Without embarrassment, the students asked significant questions and made careful observations. I learned so much that I altered my schedule and went back the next day for the lesson on the female reproductive system.

When I complimented the young teacher for her maturity and her teaching ability, she admitted that she used the overhead projector so she could turn off the lights. Her face had been red throughout. The teachers may be as shy as the parents, but at least they are tackling the problem.

Units on reproductive systems and sex habits are also being incorporated into health classes, which are required in many states as companion classes to physical education. Until some recent federal legislation, these classes were sex-segregated. In some states, physical education teachers are now being required to complete certification in health and hygiene so they will be competent to handle the issues.

All this can be summarized in a few short sentences. Teenage sex is a problem wherever people convene. Schools are doing the best they can with some solid, worthwhile, formal programs. However, parents must realize that these formal educational programs can treat human sexuality from an informative position only. They can deal only in the facts. The values are going to have to come from somewhere else. Some students may be able to make the transfer from fact to application in living, but many can't. If your child is to learn to appreciate the wonders of his own body and to guard himself against impurities of flesh and thought, if he is going to have a healthy, wholesome, biblical attitude about human sexuality, he won't learn these things from the school. There are only two other possible teachers—the church or the parents.

Alcohol

Although alcohol is a drug—actually, the most abused drug in this country—I have chosen to treat it in a different section because the schools and society treat it differently. As I pointed out earlier, in recent years drug usage has appeared to lose its appeal to many of our young people. It is no longer "cool" to take drugs. But this isn't the case with alcohol. As the use of other drugs has diminished, teenage alcohol consumption has increased. Recently, I asked a student his estimate of drug users in his suburban high school. He reported, "No more than 20 percent." I then asked his estimate of alcohol users. He reported, "More than 70 percent."

For the adolescent, alcohol is more readily available and is more socially acceptable. But it is still a drug and needs to be treated as one.

This problem is demonstrated by recent statistics. In the Gallup Poll of the public's attitude toward the public schools as published in the *Phi Delta Kappan* (September 1979), 13 percent considered the use of drugs to be the biggest problem with which the public schools must deal. This ranked as the second most frequently mentioned problem (24 percent of the population surveyed considered lack of discipline to be the biggest problem). Yet, only 2 percent of the population considered the use of alcohol as the major problem in schools.

In my opinion, the distinction between the two categories is a matter of concern. As I said before, alcohol is a drug and needs to be treated as one. While the scientists are still trying to document the dangers of some drugs, we already know the dangers of alcohol. There is no mystery here. There is no need for us to try to deceive ourselves. Teenage alcoholism is a reality. We cannot afford to take a soft stand on this problem simply because society is willing to treat it differently from any other drug problem.

The Risk. Since I do equate alcohol with other forms of drugs, I begin this discussion with the same presupposition—that for the teenager consumption in any amount is dangerous. I realize that may be an old-fashioned notion, and this evaluation may in itself be part of the problem. I realize that there are few models of total abstinence in a child's life.

The adolescent years are at best tenuous and precarious. I just don't see the wisdom of a young person's adding further risk by dulling his senses and judgment with drink. There are too many adverse possibilities—reduced academic performance, alcoholism, automobile accidents. Any young person who deals with alcohol runs the risk of damaging his life.

But young people take that chance. If your child doesn't, he will at least associate with young people who do. And he needs to know how to respond to his desires and temptations and to his own value system.

Presently, the temptations to drink are somewhat different from the temptations to experiment with other forms of drugs. For one thing, teenagers have the model question. Many of their adult models who strongly denounce drugs with appropriate fear and trembling, do drink and advertise the fact. For the teenager, drinking becomes a symbol of romantic and exciting adult behavior. Young people have an inherent need to experiment with adult behavior. You have already noticed this when your child was very young. His first games consisted of imitating adults, practicing adult behavior and adult emotions. So the teenager, when he tires of being an adolescent, might find something quite exciting and romantic and adult in going out and drinking all night. It is his way of seeing how he is going to enjoy the next phase of his development.

There is also something rather romantic in taking a chance and living through it to tell about it. In the halls of any high school, there is no greater hero than a sixteen-year-old with a newly won speeding ticket. Crowds gather rapidly and demand a blow-by-blow account of the whole ordeal. Even vicariously, those young people are thrilled with the excitement of chance. They want to take a risk, but a safe one.

Alcohol provides this safe risk. The teenagers know that there is something tantalizingly dangerous about drinking, but they perceive it must not be too dangerous because they know sane, successful adults who apparently have not been hurt by occasional nipping.

Of course, this risk taking is essential to peer acceptance. No one wants a friend who is unimaginative, bland, or cautious. So the teenager proves his social worthiness by participating in the risk.

The Defense. As a parent, what is your defense against this? The answer is rather obvious. If you don't want your child to drink, you must present him with an adult model who is cheerful and fulfilled without resorting to the deadening effects of alcohol. This model must be credible enough to convince the adolescent that the thrill doesn't justify the risk—that, in fact, the risk is greater than most adolescents think. You can tell your child all that; but if you want him to believe it, you have to *show* him. There is no other way.

But while you are showing your child this powerful model, don't forget his need to experiment with adult behavior and his need to take some risks. The solution to something as profound and frightening as your child's adolescent drinking might be as simple as your allowing him to participate in adult conversations when friends come to visit. How good is he in adult conversations? Can he carry his own, or must he learn about being an adult from his adolescent friends? This is important enough for you to invest some time in further thought.

The second piece of advice I have is for you to permit your adolescent to be an adolescent. I don't find that at all inconsistent with the above paragraph. Let him experiment with adult behavior; but at the same time, permit him some thrills, some excitment, enough risk to make him socially attractive. If you deny your son football because of the danger, make sure you have a substitute that will fulfill his inherent need to take risks. *His* choice might be a drinking spree.

But in the End, It's a Drug. I realize that these suggestions to curb the temptations of drinking in adolescents might seem superficial, but I am ready to defend them. Again, I remind you that alcohol is a drug and I urge you to apply the information on drugs in this chapter (and all the other information you have acquired about drugs) to the problem of drinking. But after you have done that, you need to ascertain the difference between the temptations of hard drugs and the temptations of alcohol. I suggest that you investigate the quality of the message of the role model and in the adolescent's perception of the risk.

A Question of Values

Despite the frightening tone, despite the various suggestions and warnings, despite the obvious complexity of the problem, the thrust of this whole chapter can be reduced to two questions. What does your child value? Where has he established his uncrossable boundaries? Notice. Those are his boundaries and not your boundaries for him. Those are boundaries which he must have in place before the temptations come. And those are boundaries that must be strong enough to hold against the forces of peer pressure, the desire to rebel against parents, and the need for youthful experimentation.

He probably established his boundaries after listening to and watching the authority figures in his life. Logically, we conclude that if you want his boundaries to be the same as yours, you must earn the right to be one of those authority figures who carry some power in his value formation. To earn that right, you must relate to your child. And now we are back to the thesis of this book.

Your ability to help your child survive and thrive in his world of school, home, friends, activities, and temptations depends on your personal relationship with him. It is easy for me to suggest that. It is also easier to talk about being a parent than it is to be one.

11

"I Forgot To Tell You, You're Supposed To Be at an Important Meeting at 6:30 Tonight."

Throughout this book, I have addressed the question of how you can help your child survive and thrive in school by focusing the discussion and suggestions on the personal or more direct perspective. I have tried to anticipate what your child, himself, might be encountering, and I have tried to suggest ways for you to help him specifically as he meets the challenges of being young.

In keeping with this perspective, I have proposed that you analyze and support schools by concentrating your efforts on the individual classroom teacher—that you know what is going on in your child's classroom, that you know how your child is responding to what is going on, that you are close enough to your child to know where the strengths and weaknesses of his school experience are, and that you and the rest of your family are prepared to fill in the gaps in your child's education.

As a veteran educator, I am happy with this focus. After my twenty years in the profession, I have concluded that each student responds to the giant institution of school in his own unique way. For some students, school is a positive institution. For some, it is negative, perhaps even destructive. From this, I have further concluded that any significant change in the quality of education will begin in individual classrooms with individual teachers.

But at the same time, I realize the inadequacy of this simple approach. There is an institution—a giant, impersonal, sometimes corrupt, sometimes unwieldy institution—called the school. Unless you have a legal alternative, your child will have to spend a minimum of 14,000 hours of his life there. It would be foolish for me to suggest that you don't need to be interested in the institution itself. If nothing more, the school is to a parent and taxpayer what a mountain is to a mountain climber. It needs to be conquered just because it is there.

Wise parents know their children. They know what is happening to their own children in the classroom, but thorough parents also know something about the institution of school as well. And this takes some attention, some study. For this reason, I conclude the book with this chapter introducing you to some of the present concerns of those people charged with the task of directing the institution. Let me emphasize the word *introduce*. Actually, I am really only going to mention these concerns. I don't promise to mention all possible concerns. In this short space, I am not going to present enough information for you to make a decision about any one of them. However, I would like to stimulate your interest.

A Warning.   I do have one note of caution which probably reflects my bias. If you decide to be a school reformer, if you decide to carry banners, publish material, lead parades, plan demonstrations, disrupt the school board meeting, or beat on administrators' doors, do it for the right reasons. Make sure that in all your efforts to make the world a better place, your primary motive is to help your own child. Don't make the mistake of getting so wrapped up in provoking change that you forget to be a parent, you forget to talk to your child, to help him read, to watch him play sports or music, to host his friends.

A Matter of Politics

I enjoy walking past elementary schools when students are dismissed in the afternoon. I enjoy watching the children and listening to their spontaneous, serious conversations. During these moments, I see purity and innocence, fervor and excitement, logic and immaturity. But I am shocked back into reality when I remember that frequent decisions affecting the quality of these young lives are made by cigar-chomping, foot-stomping, hand-banging, wheeling, dealing politicians. There is something incongruous between the innocence of the playground and the maneuver and compromise of the smoke-filled committee rooms. But that is the way it is.

Politicians decide whether those children walk to school or ride the bus. They decide what courses the children take, how many classmates they have, what college courses the teacher took, and what the children can and cannot buy to eat during school hours.

Remember, I am not evaluating this. I am simply mentioning it to make the point that most decisions affecting school life are political decisions. As such, those decisions germinate and grow like other political decisions. Voters, those are people like you, create noise. Politicians—after appropriate argument, consideration, and compromise—respond; and there is a new school law that requires your child to take Physical Education each day or prevents him from buying potato chips. This is how the system works.

I emphasize this to remind you that if you want to effect change, you must be prepared to fight political battles. But let me assure you, you can, in fact, win. Many people just like you have won.

One winter, I had to drive on a famous national highway each morning on my way to work. I began to notice the small children walking along that busy, dangerous highway on their way to school. I also noticed that buses with empty seats whizzed right past those children. That didn't seem right to me; so in a moment of unusual civic nobility, I decided to investigate.

I went to the principal, and he explained the state law. The school could legally transport children who lived more than one and a half miles from the building. In fact, that state would give the district money to transport those children. But the state wouldn't pay for students who lived within a mile and a half, thus the walkers. The principal was kind enough. He even pulled out the giant school code, blew the dust off, and let me read the law myself. All that ceremony wasn't necessary. I believed the principal, but I could tell that I wasn't going to accomplish anything here. The issue was bigger than local school policy. By then, I was so charged with the joy of civic duty that I decided to carry the issue further. I convinced the local newspaper editor to get involved. He took some pictures of those buses whizzing by the children, and he wrote some persuasive editorials. Parents began to respond. There was a letter campaign to state legislators. Before spring came, there was a rider attached to the state law that said the state would pay for transporting a child who lived within a mile and a half if the child's route to school was dangerous. Since the highway in question is as dangerous as it is famous, those children rode the bus.

I don't take the credit for this rider, but I want you to see how the process works. I want you to have confidence that it *does* work, and it works when intelligent people like you make it work. Let me list some of the issues which are presently requiring political debate and subsequent decisions. You may get excited about one of these.

School Finances.   If your school is typical, it is in financial trouble. Notice how I can make such a general statement without any specific evidence to back it up. I don't profess to be a prophet, but most schools are in some kind of financial squeeze. Such things are in vogue.

The reason for financial trouble is simple: Costs have gone up more rapidly than income. The solution to the financial woes is to find more income or reduce the costs of education. With economic brilliance like that, I should be president. Putting this brilliant theory into practice is the difficult part, so I will leave that to your school board and you.

Despite what some people think, rising costs are not necessarily the result of increased waste. Inflation has hit the school budget. During one school year in the last decade, the cost of paper tripled. Schools buy gasoline at the same price as you. During the last ten years, cost-of-living raises in salaries have literally destroyed school budgeting theory. Salaries now take as much as 25 percent more of the school budget than they did ten years ago. Let me emphasize that these are *cost-of-living raises.* Teachers have no more buying power now than they did ten years ago.

One alternative solution to the financial difficulties is to find the money to meet these rising costs. There are two possibilities—raise taxes or charge the parents for some of the school's services.

Raising taxes is not a popular idea, particularly in states like California and Massachusetts where voters have recently passed propositions to freeze or lower local taxes. Apparently, these taxpayer revolts are going to spread to other states. If you have not already, you will probably in the near future, have to make a decision about whether the schools in your state or area should have more money. Are you prepared to vote on that issue? Let's check with a short examination.

- What kind of tax is used to finance your school?
- What is the annual per-pupil expenditure in your district?
- How much of that do you pay with your taxes?

- How much surplus money does your school have? How much does it need?
- How much money does your school district receive from the state for every day your child is in school? (This is something you need to know before you plan that trip and pull your child out of school for a week.)
- What is the pay schedule for teachers in your district?

If you have the answer to all (or even most) of those questions you are now in a position to decide whether raising taxes is a possible solution to the financial problems in your district. If not, don't feel guilty; most people, even the educators, wouldn't be able to answer all these questions. But I want to make the point that sometimes we are asked to vote on crucial issues even though we may not have as much information as we need.

The second possibility for meeting rising costs is to ask the parents to pay for some of the services. Some districts have already implemented this procedure. If parents want their children to have a band, the parents must help pay the band director. If parents want their children to play football, they must help pay for the program. I know of districts where this is working well. But it does seem to contradict the American principle of free, public education, and there may be legal problems if some parents protest.

The second alternative solution to the financial difficulty of schools is to cut educational costs, and this means to cut educational services. There are several possibilities such as:

- Eliminate or reduce extracurricular activities.
- Eliminate special programs such as special education, programs for the gifted, and enriched courses with lower enrollment.
- Increase class size. (If an elementary school increased maximum class size from thirty to thirty-five, the school could reduce its staff by almost 10 percent.)

- Close schools. (Packed buildings are more economically efficient.)

It is easy for me to list these possibilities, but choosing one to implement is another matter. Implementing any one of these will greatly mar the education of some students. But if this is the alternative, someone has to make a decision. And your school board may be looking at such decisions right now. If so, those members need some suggestions from you. How important are the extracurricular activities to you and your child? Are you willing to give up your neighborhood building in order to keep art teachers in the elementary school? How should the school handle the children with learning disabilities? (That question is even more important when you have a child with learning disabilities.) If the class size increases, are you willing to make up for the loss of personal attention your child is going to suffer?

If your district is typical, these questions are relevant. The financial problem is a crucial one. Are you prepared to be a part of the solution?

Teacher Organization. Teachers have had some kind of a national organization since shortly after the Civil War. Presently, there are two major choices—the American Federation of Teachers, which is a labor union, and the National Education Association, which is the historical professional association. Although both organizations like to enumerate the differences between the two, for the taxpayer and parent they are more alike than different. Both are national umbrella organizations with state and local groups underneath. Both have made major contributions to improving the teaching profession. Both provide professional and personal services for their members.

But in recent years, the teacher organizations have assumed a new role in our society. In most states, teachers have won the right to collective bargaining or negotiation. In those states, teachers in a given district are represented by one of the two organizations, and the local teachers have the power of organization behind them when they negotiate for higher salaries or better working conditions.

The process works about the same as it does in any other labor (teachers)-management (administrators and board) relationship. Labor presents a proposed contract; management presents an alternative; hassle follows. If an agreement is reached, school continues. If not, the teachers strike. It is all rather commonplace now.

But the procedure may not be as harmless as it appears on the surface. I am convinced that any labor-management dispute will eventually be reflected in the product; and when that dispute occurs in the schools, that product is your child. We have not had the negotiation process long enough for us to determine the educational effects of bargaining and subsequent strikes, but there are some possible dangers that bear watching (without even mentioning the obvious problems that strikes create for students).

For one thing, collective bargaining has split the profession. There is definitely a "them and us" attitude among administrators and teachers. These people work in the same building, embrace the same goals and objectives, are paid from the same tax base, deal with the same children, eat in the same lunch room, and smoke and complain in the same lounge. Yet, they are divided at contract time.

Sometimes those divisions develop into uncrossable chasms. A few years ago I visited a high school at the time of rather heated contract debates. Assistant principals (agents of the administrative management) were roaming the halls searching for students who had been dismissed from classes without proper hall passes. I witnessed the apprehension of one such young man. That high school freshman was marched back to his classroom; and the principal, still clutching the culprit, denounced the teacher's shortcomings as the entire class looked on. I don't worry about the principal or the teacher. Both are adults. They should be able to adjust to sudden outbursts of childish behavior, even when it comes from another adult. But I have often wondered if that student has ever forgotten the ordeal.

Negotiations can divide administrators and teachers and can even divide teachers into camps. When this happens, the subsequent scars do not heal quickly or easily.

I am perplexed. I am pleased with the improvements that the negotiation process has brought to the teaching profession, but I am also concerned about the possible dangers, the hurt, the scars that come from a split profession.

Is there some way that we could have the best of both worlds, improvement of the profession—the salary, the working conditions, the standards—without the injuries of division?

Minimum Competency Testing.   Educators and consumers alike have become concerned with what is an apparent decrease in learning skills and educational competence. Experts (who are sometimes called researchers) have ventured guesses (which are sometimes called research) as to why Johnny can't read and Suzie can't cipher.

One possible suspect is an animal called social promotion—the idea that students are promoted from grade to grade simply because they have spent the appropriate number of hours in a given grade level. Thus, we have students who have been promoted into high school and even graduate who cannot read, write, or do arithmetic.

The obvious solution to this problem is to check the student's progress at various times during his academic career to see whether he has acquired the requisite tools. Educators all across the nation are now busy developing "minimum competency tests" to check to see if a student is fit to be promoted to the next level of work or is fit to be a high school graduate.

Some states already require such testing. Others are looking at such state legislation. Meanwhile, many local districts have developed their own standards and examinations. Consequently, minimum competency testing is now one of the most popular topics at professional meetings and in professional journals.

As I said earlier, this seems to be the obvious solution to a rather disturbing problem. But, as usual, implementing the theory has brought some controversy. Some parents claim that the tests are unfair, that they are written with an ethnic or middle-class bias. Others maintain that if the student spends his time in school, he should receive the privileges reserved for graduates. If he didn't learn anything, the school is at fault; and he shouldn't be punished for the incompetence of the school.

Some educators claim that the tests will lead to poorer teaching instead of better. They maintain that teachers would only be interested in having their students learn enough to pass the test. Thus, the teachers would be concerned with the minimum. They would, in educational language, "teach to the test."

Let me remind you that my original purpose was to introduce you to these topics, and this is a very superficial introduction to this very complex problem. It does concern you because your educators and your politicians are probably debating the question now. I warn you that what you have read here does not make you competent to hold court at the PTA meeting, but the literature is filled with discussions of minimum competency and standardized testing. I encourage you to investigate further. Your state legislator may need your opinion soon.

Text and Material Selection.   Notice how I saved the real controversy for last. Also notice the ambiguity of the subtitle. This is currently a hot topic. I don't want to offend any segment of my readers this near the end by taking an unpopular position (I only promised you an introduction), but this topic does provoke emotion, intense emotion, from proponents of both sides. I am not afraid of that emotion. In fact, it is probably good to feel strongly about something. But neither group can let emotions crowd out common sense and reason when something as precious as our children are involved.

The question is actually a rather simple one. Who has the right to decide what materials students will study? Traditionally educators have made those decisions almost by themselves. Some schools have solicited advice from concerned parent groups, but the final decisions have usually been made by the educators. In recent years, parents have demanded a stronger voice. These demands have come in various forms—speeches at board meetings, representation on textbook-selection committees, lawsuits, and in some cases, public demonstrations.

But while parents and educators wrestle over this problem, there is a question that must be answered first. Regardless of who selects the textbooks and other reading material, on what basis is that selection made? Do we choose books because of their quality without consideration of orthodoxy? Do we protect our children from confronting ideas or language or emotions that might be controversial or offensive? What are the criteria for making such decisions?

Whoops! I didn't intend to editorialize, but I do want to demonstrate that the issue of text selection is a many-faceted one which must be approached with knowledge and wisdom. If you have a child in school, you have already made some commitment to the issue. If you have not been personally involved in textbook selection, you have in effect stated your opinion that you are willing to let educators make those choices. If you have been involved, then you have stated your opinion that parents deserve a voice. If you believe that, then you need to know how to make your opinions count.

In studying this issue, the place for you to begin is to learn how textbooks are selected in your district. Some states have a state-adoption committee which approves all instructional materials at the state level. In other states, such decisions are left to individual districts. In some of those districts, there is a district-wide committee. Sometimes the decisions are left entirely to the individual teacher. You will need to know who selects the texts for your child; and if you are a person with common sense, you may need to get involved in the politics surrounding the textbook selections. The process needs your wise counsel.

Involvement: Putting Information into Practice

The four issues discussed above are just a few out of many that concern the people who make the educational decisions affecting your child. By this brief introduction, I want to make several points—these are major concerns. They merit your attention. They are complex issues that deny simple answers. They are political issues. They concern you and your child. These issues need your response.

So what can you do? First, you can make yourself knowledgeable. Then you can put your knowledge to work.

The Parent Conference.   Perhaps the simplest and most overlooked form of parent involvement is to attend scheduled conferences with your child's teachers and counselors. If you get invited, make the effort to go. I predict that something valuable will come from the exchange. Too many parents are threatened by those invitations to come to school. Those don't always mean bad news. Don't let the invitations or the school personnel put you on the defensive. You have paid for a part of that school. You have a right to be there. If you have questions, ask them. If you have suggestions, make them. School personnel are plagued by lack of parent interest. Show the teacher that at least you are interested. It will make his day.

Volunteer Teacher. Once you get confident about visiting the teacher, you may want to volunteer a few hours each week to work at school. Many schools are using parent volunteers effectively in a variety of functions. You may listen to students read, or help put up bulletin boards, or supervise the playground. But you will be doing important work, and you will be learning more about your child's school and what goes on in his life each day.

School Board. When you become confident in the school building, you may want to start attending board meetings. Such meetings are open. Why don't you attend to find out what issues concern those officials elected to run your school? Better yet, why don't you attend to let those officials know that they can depend on you? Don't be afraid to go. You won't need a special invitation or a ticket. Just call the local school and ask when the meeting is. No one will embarrass you. The board can close the meeting during discussion of personnel, but if so someone will politely ask you to leave.

Most school boards have more work to do than they can get done. Remember that these people serve for no salary and have other careers themselves. In the case of too much work, many boards have relied on special task forces composed of private, interested citizens. If you have attended board meetings a few times, you may be asked to serve. Serving in such a capacity will give you the opportunity to learn about the major issues and will let you see how decisions are made.

If you don't think your board is doing a good job, apply. Any legal voter is eligible. All you need is a small filing fee, time to campaign, and an acute interest in serving children. Don't excuse yourself on the grounds that you haven't been trained. Neither has anyone else. There are no special courses to take. Just get involved.

If you get elected, you may wish at times that you had surrendered your life to something easier, such as being a missionary to an isolated tribe in the Amazon Valley. School board members receive no monetary compensation and very few kind words. They are available to the public for advice (mostly unsolicited and not usable), and they are constantly criticized. Consequently, many districts do not have their best talent on their school boards. I urge you to take up the cause yourself; but if you don't see yourself in such a role, at least make some contribution to the mental well-being of those who do serve.

The Legislators.   You can also be a direct influence on state and federal law. Every congressman and every senator has a mailbox; and despite the rumors to the contrary, every one of them can read. Acquaint yourself with the issues. Think about the possible consequences of a piece of legislation. Then write your congressman. Your letter may be the soundest piece of advice he gets on that particular issue. Your message is important; your insight, if it originates in the Spirit of the Living God, is precious. Make yourself heard.

Your Child: Where You and the School Meet

But as you become involved at the school, district, state, or federal level, don't forget the principal character in all this effort—your child. Despite all your other accomplishments and all the other great contributions you are making to the history of mankind, your child is the one contribution that will most nearly represent what you have lived for. Such a significant contribution deserves your time, your study, your attention, and your best effort.

To complicate the situation, you are not alone in this endeavor of bringing your child through the pitfalls and promises of childhood to meaningful adulthood. Because of the nature of our society, you must entrust some of that responsibility to the school and to society itself.

Your role as a parent is to coordinate all the child's experiences into one unified, consistent, teaching agent. The difficult work here is to coordinate, not control. Parenthood would be a less frustrating, if not easier, enterprise if we could just control what our children encounter, eliminating all the negative and harmful. Since we can't do that even if we want to, we must settle for the task of coordinating.

While your child is in school, he will be under the direct supervision and influence of more than forty different adult authorities. During that time, he will also be subjected to the power of scores of his peers. Obviously, some of these people are going to contradict your suggestions. Some will contradict each other. Some will contradict your child's own value and knowledge systems. But these contradictions won't do much damage as long as your child has a stable, consistent, understanding, sensitive touchstone to help him evaluate, integrate, and unify these diverse sources and experiences. That's what parents are for, to be that touchstone, to have a close enough relationship with their child to provide stability in his life.

Let me conclude on a positive note. After having studied the educational scene firsthand for all these years, I am convinced that your child can survive and even thrive in school. Thousands do. Although he might even make it by himself, it would be easier for him if he doesn't have to tackle the task alone. And who knows, helping your son or daughter through the mysteries of school and school relationships might become some of the most memorable and rewarding moments of parenthood. You may make some lifelong friends. You may discover some dedicated,

Glossary of School Terms

Educators frequently use familiar terms but with specialized meanings. This is called "territorializing." It helps the specialist's ego, but it doesn't do much for the parent, particularly the one who doesn't understand the term. For you, I include this glossary of some of those terms. During your next conversation with an educator, nod acknowledgment occasionally; and you will disarm him completely.

Accountability. The idea, popular in the early 1970s, that schools should be accountable in hard, measurable terms for the money they spend. This movement turned evaluation of schools and classes from the process to the product—the final result, or goal.

Achievement Tests. Tests designed to measure what the student has actually learned or mastered—contrasted with tests that measure his native ability to learn.

ADA (Average Daily Attendance). In most states, this is the figure that designates the actual size of the school (rather than ADM, average daily membership). It is the average number of students present day by day. Appropriation of funds is usually based on ADA. Thus, if you keep your child home, the school loses money.

Ad Valorem Tax. A Latin term for tax based on the value, the

181

theory behind property tax assessed according to the value of the property itself.

AFT (American Federation of Teachers).   This is the teacher's union.

Alternative schools.   Some students cannot adjust to the typical school regime. For the more fortunate of these, there are alternative schools which can adjust their programs to meet the needs of those students. In some districts, alternative schools are tax supported, but this is not common.

Aptitude test.   A test that measures a student's capabilities and interests in specific activities. Counselors use results for career advising.

Assessed evaluation.   This is the value of your property as recorded on the tax roles. It may or may not be market value, depending on law and school needs. The sum of all the assessed evaluation in the district provides financial people with an operative figure for determining tax rate.

Behavioral modification.   A technique of classroom control. The student is reinforced or rewarded for his good behavior, so he repeats it until good behavior becomes his pattern. This is not always as simple as it sounds. The mystery lies in determining what is positive reinforcement for each individual student.

Behavioral objective.   A form of teachers' objectives based on the definition of *learning* as "a change in behavior." The behavioral objective must be quantifiable and measurable; so the teacher, the student, and all interested parties will know exactly what has been done and how much the student has learned. "The students will appreciate William Shakespeare" is not a behavioral objective because appreciation cannot be measured. "The students will list ten plays written by Shakespeare" is a behavioral objective. Behavioral objectives are required in some states and in some districts.

Bilingual education. This is the catchall word given to all attempts to educate the non-English-speaking students in our schools. Since this is a trend of the last ten years, bilingual educators do not agree on the proper way to tackle this problem: but in most places, teachers use the student's native language only enough to get him started in the regular English curriculum.

Bond issue. When the district needs more money, it must sell indebtedness bonds. In most cases, the schools cannot put the district into debt without permission of the voters: thus, bond issue, bond election, or referendum. In some states, schools cannot borrow money except for capital expenditures (buildings and improvements), but in other states they can borrow for regular school operations.

Brown* vs. *Board of Education Topeka, 1954. This was the Supreme Court decision that overturned the prior decision of separate but equal schools for races. In *Brown* vs. *Board of Education,* the Court ruled that schools must desegregate.

Career development. In many high schools, this is the name given to the programs designed for students who will not receive any formal education after high school graduation. (They are frequently called terminal students, a rather insensitive title at best.)

Certified teacher. A certified teacher has been licensed by the state to teach specific courses in that state. Certification requirements vary, but usually include a college degree, a specified number of courses in the field of concentration, and some courses in teaching, including an internship (student teaching). In most states a teacher is certified in either elementary (K-9, for example) or secondary (6-12, for example). Notice the indecision about who should teach the critical grades of six through nine.

Core curriculum.   Based on the idea that all human knowledge is related, this practice combines certain subjects or disciplines. The combination of language arts and social studies is the most popular core combination, but Huey in chapter two was a true core advocate.

Cross-age tutoring.   A pretentious name for an age-old practice—letting older students help tutor younger ones. This is usually good education for both the older one who teaches and the younger one who is taught.

Departmentalization.   The practice of sending students to different teachers for different content (to the math teacher for math, to the English teacher for English, and so on). Departmentalization has the advantage of letting each teacher work in the area of his strength, but it has the disadvantage of disorienting the student with too many teachers. At what age departmentalization becomes sound education is a debatable question.

Discovery or inquiry learning.   The practice of arranging problems, laboratories, or projects in such a way that the student discovers information for himself rather than being told by the teacher. The student is active rather than passive in the learning process.

Due process.   Based on the American principle that everybody is entitled to his day in court, every decision regarding your child is subject to appeal. The school should have—must have, legally—an appeal process.

Executive session.   School board meetings are open, but the board may go into executive or closed session. The board is limited by law to subjects of discussion in executive session. Matters regarding personnel, for example, are usually discussed in executive session.

Hidden curriculum. The lessons that the student learns from the structure of the school rather than from specific or overt teaching.

I.E.P. (*Individualized Education Program*). Requirement of the new federal education law (*see* Public Law 94-142). For each special-education student, the school must develop an individual program designed to meet his specific needs.

Individualized instruction. There is a broad use of this term, but generally it suggests that the student is working alone on material geared to his ability and needs.

In-house suspension. (This has other names in schools that specialize in creative titles.) Disruptive students are suspended from the normal school routine and are assigned to a special room where they sit throughout the day without the thrill of associating with their colleagues or participating in classes. Formerly, suspended students were barred from the school for the duration of their sentence, but sentencing students to holidays didn't seem to be effective punishment.

Intelligence test. A test designed to measure a student's native ability to learn—contrasted with an achievement test.

45-15 school year. Particularly in rapidly growing areas, some schools have designed a new school year that permits greater utilization of facilities. School is open throughout the whole year. Students attend classes for forty-five school days, then go on vacation for fifteen. No more than 75 percent of the school population is using the facilities at one given time. For the student and his family, vacations may fall in the winter as well as in the summer. (But I still don't understand who is available to help the farmer harvest his crops, the original purpose of the traditional summer vacation.)

Magic circle. A favorite activity of self-unfoldment educators. Students sit in the circle and discuss their feelings without fear of censorship or evaluation.

Mainstreaming. The practice of keeping special education students in regular classes and regular programs as much as possible. This is also called "least restrictive environment."

Mastery teaching. A rather recent theory, this is based on the idea that the teacher's basic role is to teach and not to evaluate. The teacher specifies the skills to be learned. The student should then be encouraged to master every one of them, and he should be given the opportunity to work on the skills until he has mastered them.

Merit pay. Based on the notion that good teachers should be paid more just for being good. The problem lies in deciding who is a good teacher and deserves the merit. Presently, most salary schedules reward years of experience and advanced degrees.

Middle school. In many instances, nothing more than a fancy name for a junior high school. But in the beginning, the middle-school concept was based on several distinct educational principles including: grades 6-8 student body rather than the traditional 7-9 division, flexible grouping, and team-teaching groups.

Mile and one-half limit. In most states, the state will reimburse the district for transporting students who live farther than one and a half miles from the school building.

Mill levy. A mill is a unit of money—one tenth of a penny or the value of a trading stamp. Sometimes this unit is used to fix the rate of taxation of assessed property. In some states, taxpayers have the opportunity to vote on the amount of mills assessed for school budget needs.

Minimum competency testing. The idea that a student should verify by examination that he has mastered the minimum skills and knowledge of one level of education before he is promoted to the next level.

Modular scheduling. This term is used to designate any variation of the traditional sixty-minute class period. Some schools employ a complex system with a series of fifteen-minute modules permitting a range of flexibility for class time (for example, lab classes take longer).

N.D.E.A. (National Defense Education Act). Of Sputnik vintage, this act provided for federal financial aid for specific school programs. Originally, its major thrust was in math and science, but the program has been extended to include almost every area of public schools, including college loans to future teachers.

NEA (National Education Association). (State and local units use similar names.) A professional teacher's organization which has served teachers for more than 100 years. This organization has a strong national lobby.

Negotiable item. In teacher-board negotiations, some items of school business are subject to negotiation, but some, such as length of school year, are not.

Old Deluder Satan Act of 1647. (I just threw this in to impress you with my knowledge of educational history.) The first significant piece of educational legislation, this Massachusetts colony law required that any community of fifty families must maintain a school. The purpose of education was to thwart Satan's efforts.

Packaged-learning modules. In an individualized educational program, each student receives an individual package of learning materials and activities. Ideally, this package has been selected specifically for him. Some schools rely on the computer to make these selections. See Kinner in chapter two.

Peer tutoring. Letting one child help another of the same age with his studies. Notice how educators can assign impressive titles to almost any human function.

Percentile score. An understandable means for reporting standardized test scores. A percentile score indicates what percentage of the population scored below that student. A percentile score of 76 means that the student scored higher than 76 percent of the test population. He is in the top one-fourth.

Per-pupil expenditure. The amount of money the school spends to educate one child for a year. The figure is ascertained by dividing the total budget by the number of students. It is a useful piece of information.

Precision teaching. A relatively new (and rather localized) approach to skill teaching. In precision teaching, each student is measured to determine his ability to perform certain learning activities. During the learning activities, he then works against himself and his own rate of performance.

Public Law 94-142. A federal, special-education law, it requires that a district is responsible for meeting the individual educational needs of every student, regardless of the student's limitations.

Regional accreditation. In the United States, there are eight regional accreditation agencies that equalize school standards and then accredit the schools which can meet these standards. Since these agencies accredit schools at every level of the school ladder, from elementary through higher education, accreditation does suggest a certain level of quality. Frequently, the standard of the regional agencies are significantly higher than state standards, so there is some prestige.

Self-contained classroom.   A classroom where the child spends most of his day and receives his instruction in all subjects from one teacher. Modified self-contained classrooms allow for the student to leave his teacher for very specialized programs such as music and physical education.

Sports Illustrated.   The unofficial, school administrators' professional journal. If your principal appears grumpy, check to see if his subscription has expired.

Staffing.   In some locales this term applies to the activity of calling together all interested parties to discuss a child's progress. The meeting includes his teachers, the counselor, the principal, parents, and specialized personnel who have an interest.

Standardized test.   A test given to a broad population. Results are compiled and standardized by use of the normal distribution scale. Thus, a student can know how his score compared with a national average. Standardized tests are used widely in determining a school's effectiveness and in predicting a student's success in the next level of education. They are also used by classroom teachers when the teacher wants to know how his students compare with other students across the nation, or when the teacher is too lazy to write his own test.

Teaching simulations.   A rather new and popular activity based on the theory that students learn by participation. Real situations are simulated to be used in the classroom format, and students play the parts. For example, an eighth-grade class spends several days each spring simulating the national congress with students playing strategic roles in making national decisions.

Team teaching.   When teachers share responsibilities for a given class. Although this term has broad usage and is not always practiced in its purest form, team teaching is based on the idea that a teacher should be permitted to spend most of his time performing those activities he is good at. Lecturers should lecture; helpers should help.

Tenure. After a teacher has taught in one district for a given number of years, he is given some job security.

Titles. The NDEA funds were distributed through a series of titles.

Title IX. The nondiscrimination law. Because of this, many schools have made their physical education classes coeducational, spent more money on women's sports, and eliminated sex requirements in certain courses.